BrandNameS
Built on Standards

How Brands Are Designed, Built, and Trusted Online

BNS Publishing

ISBN: 978-0-9834193-5-8

CONTENTS

DEDICATION

To every entrepreneur, creative professional and business leader
who refuses to let their brand fade into obscurity.
To those who understand that a strong digital presence
is not a luxury—it's a necessity.

ACKNOWLEDGMENTS

Every book has a story behind it — and this one carries the strength, effort, discipline, and vision of the people who believed in the mission long before a single chapter was written.

To everyone who supported this work, encouraged its development, and trusted the BrandNameSites philosophy from the beginning: thank you. Your belief made this possible.

To our family and loved ones — thank you for giving us the space, time, and focus to build something meaningful. Your patience and encouragement made the long days and late nights worth it.

To every small business owner, every creative, every entrepreneur, and every dreamer who has ever said, "I just want clarity" — you are the reason this book exists. Your struggles, questions, and determination shaped the structure of this framework. Your courage to build something of your own is the heartbeat of BrandNameSites.

To the clients who trusted us with their brands: you allowed us to test, refine, and perfect these standards in the real world. You helped us turn experience into wisdom and wisdom into a system that others can now follow.

To the branding and web community: thank you for pushing the industry forward, inspiring higher standards, and motivating us to be better, smarter, and more intentional every year.

And finally, to those who will use this book to transform their brand, improve their presence, and raise their standards — you're not just reading a book. You're building the next chapter of your business. And we're honored to be a part of that journey with you.

Thank you for believing in clarity.
Thank you for committing to consistency.
Thank you for choosing discipline over chaos.
Thank you for setting the standard.

This is only the beginning

INTRODUCTION

Modern branding has reached a point where everyone seems to have an opinion, but very few people have a standard. Businesses are told to "build a brand," "post content," "create a website," "find your voice," and "get online"—all while trying to keep up with trends that change every few months. It's no surprise that many entrepreneurs feel lost. Information is everywhere, but guidance is scattered, contradictory, and often outdated.

For the past decade, branding advice has barely evolved. You hear the same instructions on repeat: choose your colors, get a logo, post consistently. Meanwhile, the digital world has completely changed how people discover, evaluate, and trust businesses. Your website, your content, and your online behavior now shape your reputation long before a customer ever speaks to you.

Yet most branding guidance still comes from a world before smartphones, social media, and search algorithms—before your website became the centerpiece of your business. This disconnect leaves business owners piecing together advice from multiple sources, unsure of what matters and what doesn't, doing their best with rules that no longer apply.

This book exists to solve that gap.

This is the modern foundation—the standard—for what every serious brand must understand about competing in today's digital economy. We've taken the most important principles of branding, paired them with digital reality, and distilled them into a system that is clear, complete, and simple to use.

Our goal is simple:
To give you the clarity, structure, and confidence to build a brand that lasts—both online and off.

Whether you're new to business, rebranding, or strengthening what you already built, this book will help you understand:

- What branding actually means today

- The pillars every strong brand must stand on

- How to create a consistent and memorable identity

- What your website must have to build trust

- How to maintain your digital presence long-term

- How content shapes reputation and visibility

- Where brands fail—and how to avoid those mistakes

Most importantly, this book is written for real people. No buzzwords. No marketing fluff. No unnecessary complexity. Just the truth, the standards, and the steps.

Consider it your compass in a crowded digital landscape. A guide created to help you move with intention, design with clarity, and show up online with excellence.

THE OUTDATED PROBLEM WITH BRANDING ADVICE

For years, branding advice has been recycled without anyone stopping to ask if it still applies. Most traditional books focus on aesthetics—logos, colors, fonts—or broad theories like archetypes and personality matrices. Helpful, yes, but only a small fraction of what it takes to build a modern brand—like polishing your business card while your website is somewhere screaming for help.

What's missing is the *operational* side of branding.
How does your brand translate into a website that converts?
How do you stay consistent across every digital platform?
How do you build trust in a world where customers have infinite choices and a three-second attention span?

Older branding models weren't built for mobile-first design, UX standards, social media behavior, search engines, online reviews, or fast-moving digital expectations. They weren't built for an era where most customers interact with your brand online before they ever see it in person.

That's why so many businesses are working hard and still not seeing results— they're using outdated rules in a modern game.

This book retires those outdated rules and replaces them with direction built for the world we actually live in.

THE MISSING PIECE: MODERN ONLINE PRESENCE

Most branding conversations obsess over visuals. But visuals alone don't carry your brand anymore—your online presence does.

Your brand no longer lives on a business card, storefront, or brochure. **It lives online.**

Customers judge your brand through:

- Your website

- Your content

- Your digital behavior

- Your consistency

- Your clarity

- Your tone, visuals, and message across every platform

Your online presence is the version of your business people interact with when you're asleep, busy, or unavailable. It's where reputations are formed and trust is either strengthened or destroyed.

But because traditional branding never focused on digital performance, most brands treat their online presence as an afterthought. This book puts it exactly where it belongs—at the center.

Your digital presence is not optional. It's the primary way you're judged, chosen, trusted, or dismissed. And until now, most branding books have ignored it.

WHY STANDARDS MATTER

In a world where anyone can start a business in minutes, the difference between brands that thrive and brands that struggle often comes down to one thing:

Standards.

Standards give your business structure.
They eliminate guesswork.
They create consistency.
They build trust.
They help your brand feel intentional, recognizable, and reliable.

Without standards, brands become scattered. The website looks one way. Social media looks another. Messaging shifts constantly. Customers feel the inconsistency—even if they can't explain it—and walk away.

With standards, everything aligns.
Your brand moves as one system.
Every part reinforces the next.
Your identity becomes unmistakable.

Most small businesses lack standards not because they don't care, but because no one ever gave them a modern framework. This book gives you that framework.

HOW TO USE THIS BOOK

This book was designed to be practical and easy to apply. Think of it as your roadmap—a manual you'll return to again and again as your business grows.

Here's the best way to use it:

1. **Start from the beginning.**
   Branding builds in layers. The first chapters give you the foundation needed for everything else.

2. **Read with your business in mind.**
   Apply what you learn immediately. Notice what aligns, what needs fixing, and what needs redefining.

3. **Use the worksheets as tools.**
   They're here to support clarity—not overwhelm you.

4. **Revisit sections as your brand evolves.**
   Your business will change. This book is designed to grow with you.

5. **Fix one major area at a time.**
   You don't need to perfect everything at once. Small, strategic improvements compound into brand strength.

6. **Treat this as your standard.**
   Not inspiration. Not theory. A playbook for building and maintaining a modern brand.

7. **Return to it often.**
   Your first read-through gives clarity.
   Your second gives confidence.
   Your third gives mastery.

THE BRANDNAMESITES PROMISE

When we created this book, we made a promise to ourselves—and to you:

This will be the only book you need to understand branding and online presence in today's world.

Not one of many.
Not another opinion.
Not recycled advice.
A complete, modern system.

Other books talk about branding from the perspective of design, marketing, or psychology. But today's brands live in an interconnected digital ecosystem—and no single discipline can stand alone.

Your brand identity, your website, your content, your visuals, and your digital behavior are all part of one system. When one weakens, the others suffer.

So we built a system that strengthens all of them—together.

A system where:

- Your brand identity guides your decisions
- Your website becomes your digital home
- Your content reinforces your message
- Your visuals support your credibility
- Your digital behavior builds trust
- Your standards protect your consistency

This is the system we use in our own work.
The system we use with clients.
The system that turns scattered brands into organized ones—and invisible brands into respected, trusted ones.

By the time you finish this book, you'll know how to build a brand that feels strong, looks consistent, and performs with clarity across every digital platform.

No guesswork.
No confusion.
No outdated advice.
Just a complete, integrated, modern standard.

We didn't write this book to impress anyone.
We wrote it to equip you—to give you the blueprint, the clarity, and the confidence to build something real, lasting, and undeniably yours.

That's the BrandNameSites promise.

PART 1 – FOUNDATIONS OF MODERN BRANDING

WHAT BRANDING ACTUALLY IS (NOT WHAT SOCIAL MEDIA SAYS)

Branding has become one of the most misunderstood concepts in business. Everywhere you look, someone is promoting a new method, shortcut, or trend that promises to "instantly elevate" your business. The problem is that most of this advice comes from surface-level thinking, quick-fix culture, or people whose only experience with "branding" is choosing fonts and posting on Instagram.

Social media has made branding look like a collection of pretty things—matching posts, trendy fonts, polished photos, and nice colors.

But branding is not decoration.
Branding is direction.

Branding is not how your business *looks*.
Branding is how your business *lives*—in the mind, in the heart, and in the experience of the people you serve.

To understand branding the right way, we first need to separate what it *isn't* from what it actually *is*.

WHAT BRANDING IS NOT

Branding Is NOT a Logo

A logo is a symbol.
Branding is the meaning behind that symbol.

A logo identifies your business.
Branding defines your business.

A logo is seen.
Branding is felt.

Your logo is similar to a person's name—it helps people recognize you, but it doesn't reveal your values, your personality, your consistency, or the experience you offer. Many businesses assume that once a logo is created, the brand is complete. In reality, a logo without a brand behind it is just a graphic. A beautifully designed symbol with no meaning behind it is like a flag with no country.

When your brand is strong, your logo gains value.
When your brand is weak, your logo becomes decoration.

Warning: A logo redesign is not a rebrand. If all you change is the artwork, you haven't transformed your brand—you've just updated your desktop wallpaper.

Branding Is NOT Marketing

Branding is who you are.
Marketing is how you communicate who you are.

Branding is internal.
Marketing is external.

Branding is long-term identity.
Marketing is short-term activity.

Marketing attracts attention.
Branding turns that attention into trust.

You can have great marketing and a weak brand—it will bring short-lived results but nothing that lasts. You can have a strong brand and weak marketing—it will create loyal fans, but growth will be slow. The best businesses have both: a strong identity expressed through strategic marketing.

Warning: More marketing does **not** fix a weak brand. Invest first in having something worth amplifying.

Branding Is NOT Aesthetic

An aesthetic is your visual style—your look, your vibe, your "feel." It matters, but it is not the brand itself. Too many entrepreneurs create beautiful designs without defining who they are, what they believe, or what makes them different. The result: a gorgeous, empty box.

Branding is the promise behind the aesthetic.
Aesthetic without strategy is decoration.
Branding with aesthetic is communication.

People don't stay loyal because something looks good.
They stay loyal because something feels right.

WHAT BRANDING ACTUALLY IS

Branding is the complete perception people have of your business—before, during, and after they interact with you. It's the combination of your visuals, voice, values, behavior, and experience working together to create trust.

If you lost every logo file, every template, and every social media post tomorrow… would your brand still exist?

If the answer is yes, you have a brand.
If the answer is no, you have design assets—not a brand.

More precisely, branding operates on three interconnected levels:

1. The Psychological Role: What People Understand About You

Your brand shapes how people *think* about your business. It sets expectations, clarifies your purpose, and positions you in their mind. A clear brand answers:

- What do we believe?
- Who do we serve?
- Why does it matter?

People use branding as a mental shortcut.
Consistency creates familiarity.
Familiarity creates trust.
Trust drives decisions.

2. The Emotional Role: What People Feel About You

Logic gets attention, but emotion drives action.

People don't buy from brands—they buy from the *way brands make them feel.* A strong brand creates alignment, connection, and confidence. It reinforces identity and builds belonging.

When people feel connected to your brand, they don't just buy—they advocate.

3. The Functional Role: What You Actually Deliver

A brand must hold up in practice.
This includes:

- systems
- service quality
- customer experience
- technology
- usability
- website performance
- communication

Your brand is reinforced (or damaged) every time a customer interacts with your business. Clear, consistent, reliable function strengthens the psychological and emotional components of your brand.

When you combine psychological clarity, emotional connection, and functional reliability, people trust you. And trust is the currency of every strong brand.

CASE ANALOGIES

Branding as a Neighborhood Reputation

A neighborhood isn't defined by the welcome sign. It's defined by how people feel walking through it—the energy, the culture, the people, the consistency. The sign is just a signal; the reputation is the reality.

Branding as a First Impression

A logo is the outfit.
Branding is the personality, presence, and feeling you create when you step into the room.

Branding as a Restaurant Experience

A menu and logo may get customers in the door, but the taste, service, and experience bring them back. Branding is the full experience—not the paper menu.

Branding as a Promise

Your logo signs the promise.
Your brand keeps it.

Additional Modern Definitions

Branding is:

- the reputation you build over time
- the promise you keep
- the personality behind your business
- the emotional impression people have after every interaction
- the reason someone chooses you instead of a competitor

Think about well-known brands like Apple or Walmart. You instantly feel something when you hear their names—innovation, simplicity, affordability, convenience. That instant emotional reaction is branding.

Your brand lives in the minds of your customers—not in your Canva folder.

INTEGRATED ROLE OF FUNCTION, EMOTION & IDENTITY

Strong brands align all three:

- **Function** (you deliver)
- **Emotion** (they feel)
- **Identity** (you're recognizable)

When one is weak, the brand is weak.

A brand with great function but no emotional connection feels forgettable.
A brand with emotion but poor function loses trust.
A brand with identity but no substance becomes all style, no credibility.

The best brands balance all three. They work. They feel right. They're instantly recognizable.

THE SIX PILLARS OF A BRAND

Every strong brand is built on a foundation. Not luck. Not trends. Not good timing. A foundation. These foundations—your brand's pillars—keep your identity consistent, believable, and trustworthy. Without them, a business ends up guessing, changing direction constantly, blending in with competitors, and confusing the very people it aims to serve.

Think of these pillars as the load-bearing walls of a building. You can change the furniture, freshen up the paint, and update the décor—but if the walls crack, the whole structure is in danger. The same applies to your brand.

These six pillars form the structure your brand needs to grow with clarity and confidence:

1. **Purpose — Why you exist**
2. **Vision — Where you're going**
3. **Values — What you stand for**
4. **Audience — Who you serve**
5. **Identity — How you show up**
6. **Experience — What people actually get**

Let's break each one down clearly.

PILLAR 1 — PURPOSE

Why You Exist

Purpose is the reason your brand exists beyond making money. It answers one powerful question:

"Why do we do what we do?"

Purpose gives your brand direction and meaning. It becomes your filter for decisions, your anchor during tough seasons, and the emotional core of why customers connect with you.

Examples

A web design company:
"We help small businesses show up professionally online so they can compete and grow."

TOMS: *"To improve lives through business."*
Patagonia: *"We're in business to save our home planet."*

Notice the pattern: purpose is not about the product. It's about the impact.

Why Purpose Matters

- It separates a **business** from a **brand**
- It attracts aligned customers
- It provides direction during uncertainty
- It motivates your team when things get challenging

Without purpose, you're just selling things. With purpose, you're building something meaningful.

Standard for Purpose

Your purpose must be:

- Short
- Clear
- Action-driven
- Connected to the people you serve
- Authentic
- Impossible for competitors to copy without sounding dishonest

If you can't say it in one sentence, it's not defined enough.

Warning

Don't confuse purpose with a tagline or slogan. Purpose isn't marketing. It's your internal compass.

PILLAR 2 — VISION

Where You're Going

Vision is the future picture of your brand—the destination you want to reach. Where purpose explains *why* you exist, vision explains *where* you're headed.

Vision answers:
"What does success look like 5–10 years from now?"

Examples

Microsoft (early days): *"A computer on every desk and in every home."*
Airbnb: *"A world where anyone can belong anywhere."*
A small agency: *"To become the trusted online branding resource for small businesses worldwide."*

These visions are vivid—not vague.

Why Vision Matters

A strong vision:

- Creates long-term direction
- Helps you prioritize
- Attracts aligned team members
- Builds internal momentum
- Prevents your brand from drifting when things get busy

Standard for Vision

Your vision must:

- Describe a future state
- Be ambitious but achievable
- Inspire your team
- Align with your purpose
- Be specific enough to guide decisions

Warning

Avoid visions that sound like corporate filler.
"Be the best."
"Lead the industry."
"Change the world."

None of these guide anything. Real visions paint a picture.

PILLAR 3 — VALUES

What You Stand For

Values are the principles that shape how your brand behaves. They guide your decisions, messaging, customer experience, and internal culture.

They answer:
"What do we believe in, and how does that affect the way we act?"

Examples of Values

- Respect
- Transparency
- Quality
- Creativity
- Service
- Consistency
- Sustainability
- Courage
- Inclusion

Real values show up in behavior—not on posters.

Why Values Matter

Values influence:

- Who you hire
- How you treat customers
- What projects you take on
- What you refuse to compromise on
- How consistent your brand feels

People can feel when your behavior doesn't match your values.

Standard for Values

Your values should:

- Guide every interaction
- Show up in your content and customer experience
- Be specific and actionable
- Reflect reality—not aspiration
- Be no more than 3–7 core principles

Warning

A value written but not lived is worse than having no values at all. Customers will call you out long before you realize the disconnect.

PILLAR 4 — AUDIENCE

Who You Serve

Your audience is the specific group of people your brand is built for—not "everyone," not "anyone who needs help," but a defined, meaningful group.

A clear brand serves a clear audience.

Examples

A small-business branding agency might focus on:

- Solo entrepreneurs
- Service providers
- Creative professionals
- Small businesses ready to scale

A personal trainer might focus on:

- Postpartum moms
- Busy professionals
- Athletes recovering from injury

Why Audience Matters

Knowing your audience:

- Sharpens your messaging
- Strengthens your visuals
- Increases conversions
- Improves content strategy
- Helps you differentiate
- Makes decision-making easier

When you speak to everyone, you connect with no one.

Standard for Audience

Define your audience by:

- Needs
- Pain points
- Behavior patterns
- Goals
- Language
- Lifestyle
- Buying triggers

You should be able to describe your ideal customer in a genuine conversation—not read them from a script.

Warning

If your audience could apply to nearly anyone, it's not defined enough.

PILLAR 5 — IDENTITY

How You Show Up

Identity is the visual and verbal expression of your brand. This includes your:

- Logo
- Colors
- Typography
- Imagery
- Voice
- Tone
- Messaging framework

Identity helps people recognize your brand in seconds. It's not about being fancy—it's about being memorable *and* aligned with your purpose, vision, values, and audience.

Examples

A professional brand may use:

- Clean fonts
- Minimal color usage
- A confident and direct voice

A creative brand may use:

- Bold colors
- Expressive visuals
- A conversational or playful tone

Why Identity Matters

Strong identity builds:

- Recognition
- Trust
- Professionalism
- Memorability

Inconsistent identity destroys all four.

Standard for Identity

Your identity must be:

- Consistent
- Easy to recognize
- True to your purpose and audience
- Simple enough to maintain long-term
- Documented in clear brand guidelines

Warning

Identity chosen only because "it's trending" becomes outdated fast. Identity built on purpose lasts.

PILLAR 6 — EXPERIENCE

What People Actually Get

Experience is how people feel when they interact with your brand. It's the most honest pillar because customers feel it instantly and remember it long after.

Experience includes:

- Customer service
- Website usability
- Content quality
- Speed and responsiveness
- Communication style
- Follow-through
- Professionalism
- Reliability

Experience is where your brand becomes real.

Examples

If your brand claims to be "simple and stress-free," then:

- Your website must be clear
- Your process must be organized
- Your communication must be easy to follow

If you promise "premium quality," then:

- Your packaging
- Your responses
- Your attention to detail
- Your post-purchase support
  All must reflect luxury.

Why Experience Matters

Identity gets attention.
Experience keeps it.

A beautiful brand with a poor experience is worse than having no brand at all.

Standard for Experience

Your experience must:

- Match your identity
- Honor your values
- Serve your audience well
- Be repeatable and reliable
- Improve over time
- Create trust

Warning

A powerful brand promise paired with a weak experience guarantees disappointment.

HOW THE SIX PILLARS WORK TOGETHER

These pillars do not operate independently—they form a unified system.

- **Purpose** explains why you exist
- **Vision** clarifies where you're going
- **Values** determine how you behave
- **Audience** defines who you're building for
- **Identity** shapes how you express yourself
- **Experience** proves everything you claim is true

When these pillars align, your brand feels strong, clear, and consistent.
When even one is misaligned, customers feel the disconnect—even if they can't explain it.

Final Thought for This Chapter

These six pillars are the structure your brand stands on. Every decision, every design choice, every piece of content, and every part of your online presence should connect back to them. Without these pillars, branding becomes guesswork. With them, your brand becomes intentional, stable, and built for long-term success.

BRAND PERSONALITY & VOICE SYSTEMS

A brand isn't just what people *see*—it's what they *hear*, too. It's how your business sounds, explains, teaches, reassures, and communicates with real people in real moments.

Most entrepreneurs obsess over visuals—fonts, logos, colors—while overlooking the part of their brand customers interact with every single day: **their voice**.

Your voice shapes perception.
Your personality shapes trust.
And both must be intentional.

Brand personality is how your business would behave if it were a person. Brand voice is how your business would sound if it were speaking out loud.

Both matter. Both create recognition. Both determine whether you feel human, trustworthy, and consistent—or scattered and forgettable.

PERSONALITY VS. TONE

Understanding the difference is where most brands go wrong.

Personality: Who You Are

Your personality is your brand's character—its internal DNA. It's long-term, rooted in your values, and doesn't change based on circumstances.

Examples of brand personality traits:

- Confident
- Supportive
- Empowering
- Practical
- Creative
- Bold
- Warm
- Direct

If your brand were a person, these traits describe how it would show up every day.

Tone: How You Speak in the Moment

Tone is the *attitude* you take depending on the situation.
Tone shifts. Personality doesn't.

Tone changes:

- A serious tone for legal communication
- A supportive tone when guiding a client
- A friendly tone when welcoming new customers
- A direct tone when giving instructions

Simple Analogy:
Your personality is who you are.
Your tone is how you respond based on the moment.

Keeping your personality consistent while adjusting tone appropriately makes your brand feel stable, trustworthy, and human.

BUILDING YOUR BRAND VOICE

A strong voice system keeps your communication consistent whether it appears on your website, social media, emails, or customer support.

Your voice should reflect:

- Your brand values
- Your audience's communication style
- Your industry positioning (traditional, modern, disruptive)
- Your internal leadership or founder personality (if founder-led)

A practical way to define your brand voice is using four key spectrums:

1. **Funny ⟵⟶ Serious**
2. **Formal ⟵⟶ Casual**
3. **Respectful ⟵⟶ Irreverent**
4. **Enthusiastic ⟵⟶ Matter-of-fact**

Where your brand lands across these determines your voice traits.

Example voice outcomes:

If you land:

- Slightly funny
- Casual
- Respectful
- Moderately enthusiastic

Your voice might be:
Friendly, conversational, optimistic, approachable.

The goal is not to sound perfect. The goal is to sound like *you*—everywhere.

MESSAGE ARCHITECTURE

Your message architecture is the backbone of what you communicate.

It keeps your messaging focused instead of sounding like a different brand every week.

A strong message architecture includes:

1. Core Message

The main idea your brand wants people to remember.

Example:
"We help businesses build a strong, clear, and professional presence online."

2. Supporting Messages

The ideas that reinforce your core message.

Examples:

- "Consistency builds trust."
- "Your website is your digital foundation."
- "Branding must be simple, clear, and structured."

3. Proof Points

Evidence that makes your message believable.

Examples:

- "Over 15 combined years of branding and digital experience."
- "Systems built from real business results."

4. Boundaries

What your brand does *not* promise.

Examples:

- "We don't guarantee overnight success."
- "We don't rely on trends or gimmicks."

Your message architecture becomes the map for every communication touchpoint—from your website to your emails to how you explain your services in person.

SIGNATURE LANGUAGE

Signature language is your brand's **verbal fingerprint**—the phrases, words, and expressions people begin to associate with you.

These create instant familiarity.

Examples (BrandNameSites Style):

- "Show up professionally online."
- "Your digital foundation."
- "Clarity creates confidence."
- "Set the standard."
- "Structure over confusion."

When people repeat your phrases, your brand has officially entered their mind.

Signature language must be:

- True to who you are
- Easy to understand
- Repeatable
- Memorable
- Consistent across platforms

You don't force signature language—it emerges from intentional repetition.

BRAND VOICE CONSISTENCY CHART

This chart helps your entire team communicate with the same personality—while adjusting tone based on context.

This chart keeps your communication flexible but consistent—critical for brand trust.

FINAL THOUGHT FOR THIS CHAPTER

A strong brand voice is not about being clever or trendy—it's about being consistent, trustworthy, and unmistakably *you.*

When your personality is clear, your tone is appropriate, your message architecture is structured, and your signature language becomes familiar, your brand becomes easy to understand and impossible to forget.

Branding is not just what people **see**.
It's what they **hear**.
And what they hear should always reinforce who you are.

VISUAL BRANDING STANDARDS

A brand's personality may be heard in its voice, but its identity is seen in its visuals.

Visual branding is the first thing people notice—your colors, your typography, your layout, your imagery. But here's the truth: **visuals should never be created first.** They must sit on top of the foundation you built in your previous chapters:
Purpose. Vision. Values. Audience. Identity.

Once those pillars are clear, your visual identity simply expresses who you already are.

Visual branding isn't about making things prettier.
It's about making things clearer, more consistent, and more recognizable.

Your visual standards protect your brand from randomness, trends, and design chaos. They ensure that no matter who creates your content— designer, assistant, intern, even you on a late night—the brand still feels like one unified voice.

Let's break down the essentials.

COLOR THEORY — THE FASTEST FORM OF COMMUNICATION

Color speaks long before your words do. People feel color immediately— trust, energy, calm, luxury, caution—often before they consciously notice it.

But choosing colors isn't just about picking pretty swatches.
Color must be strategic, emotional, and functional.

Color Roles

Every brand needs a structured palette:

- **Primary Colors** — Your core identity (1–3 colors)
- **Secondary Colors** — Supportive, flexible additions (2–4 colors)
- **Accent Colors** — Used sparingly for emphasis (1–2 colors)
- **Neutral Colors** — Grays, whites, blacks for backgrounds and text

This keeps your visuals intentional instead of chaotic.

Meaning of Common Colors

- **Blue:** Trust, calm, professionalism
- **Red:** Passion, urgency, dominance
- **Green:** Growth, nature, renewal
- **Orange:** Friendliness, energy
- **Purple:** Creativity, wisdom
- **Yellow:** Optimism, clarity
- **Black:** Luxury, power, simplicity
- **White:** Cleanliness, openness

These meanings shift by context, industry, and culture—but they anchor your emotional direction.

Color Usage: The 60–30–10 Rule

A timeless formula for balance:

- **60%** neutral or main background
- **30%** secondary color
- **10%** accent color for moments of attention

Simple. Balanced. Extremely effective.

Accessibility Standards (Non-Negotiable)

Your colors must be readable for *everyone*.
Follow WCAG contrast ratios:

- Regular text: **4.5:1**
- Large text: **3:1**
- Interactive elements: **3:1**

If your light-gray text looks "clean" but no one can read it, it's not good design—it's exclusion.

Common Mistake

Choosing colors because they are trendy, aesthetic, or "your favorite."
Visual identity must be strategic, not personal hobby art.

Standard

A strong color palette is:

- Limited (5–7 total colors)
- Balanced between bold and neutral
- Documented with hex/RGB/CMYK
- Accessible across all platforms
- Used consistently everywhere

Color is not decoration—it is communication.

TYPOGRAPHY — THE VOICE OF VISUAL DESIGN

If color sets the mood, typography sets the tone. The fonts you choose create personality, hierarchy, and readability.

Typography is often underestimated, yet nothing makes a brand look "cheap" faster than inconsistent fonts.

Components of Typography

- **Font Families** — serif, sans serif, script, display, monospace
- **Pairing** — one headline font + one body font
- **Hierarchy** — H1, H2, H3, body, captions
- **Spacing** — line-height, letter spacing
- **Weights** — bold, regular, light

Font Psychology

- **Serif fonts:** traditional, established, trustworthy
- **Sans-serif fonts:** modern, clean, digital-forward
- **Script fonts:** personal, elegant (use sparingly)
- **Display fonts:** bold, artistic (for special use)
- **Monospace fonts:** technical, precise

Your Typography System

Most brands need only:

- **1 headline font**
- **1 body font**
- **1 optional accent font**

And that's it.

Best Practices

- Body text should be **16px minimum**
- Headlines should scale down properly for mobile
- Use consistent line-height (1.4–1.6 for body texts)
- Use 2–4 font weights max
- Avoid decorative fonts for long paragraphs
- Strong contrast between fonts = strong hierarchy

Common Mistake

Using five fonts because "they looked cool."
Typography should guide, not distract.

Standard

Your typography must:

- Support your personality
- Be legible on all screens
- Be consistent across all platforms
- Use a documented hierarchy

Typography is your **visual voice**—it should speak clearly.

Spacing — The Invisible Ingredient of Premium Design

Good spacing is what makes a brand feel premium, modern, and trustworthy.
Poor spacing is what makes a brand feel crowded, cheap, or unprofessional.

Most beginners try to fill space.
Professionals know that *empty space is the luxury.*

Types of Spacing

- **White Space** — breathing room
- **Padding** — inside elements
- **Margins** — around elements
- **Line Spacing** — between lines
- **Grid Alignment** — structural order

The 8-Point Grid System

Professionals use an 8px system because:

- It's clean
- Scales beautifully
- Works across devices
- Ensures consistency

Example spacing values:
8px, 16px, 24px, 32px, 48px, 64px.

Common Mistake

Trying to fill every corner.
More space = more clarity.

Standard

If something feels off, add space.
Spacing is one of the simplest ways to elevate your brand instantly.

IMAGERY — WHAT YOUR BRAND LOOKS LIKE WITHOUT SAYING A WORD

Images build emotion faster than copy.
Your imagery should feel like it all comes from one brand—not ten different moods.

Types of Imagery

- Photography
- Icons
- Illustrations
- Graphics
- Background textures
- Patterns

Guidelines

Your imagery must be:

- High-resolution
- Consistent in lighting & tone
- On-brand in mood
- Clean and uncluttered
- Relevant to your audience

Example distinctions:

A fitness brand's imagery: energetic, bold, sweaty, high-contrast
A spa brand's imagery: soft, natural, neutral, calming
Both are correct. Both express identity.

Icon & Graphic Style

Pick ONE style:

- Line or filled
- Rounded or sharp
- Simple or detailed

And stick to it across all platforms.

Common Mistake

Using generic stock photos with staged, awkward models.
Aim for authenticity, consistency, and emotion.

BRAND KITS — YOUR VISUAL RULEBOOK

A brand kit ensures everything stays consistent—even when different people create content.

A Complete Brand Kit Includes

- Logo variations (full, stacked, icon-only)
- Color palette (hex, RGB, CMYK, Pantone)
- Typography system
- Iconography rules
- Photography style guidelines
- Spacing system
- Graphic elements (patterns, textures)
- Templates
- Usage do's and don'ts

Standard

Your brand kit must be:

- Simple to follow
- Detailed enough to maintain consistency
- Accessible to your team
- Updated as your brand evolves

A brand kit is not optional. It is your brand's visual governance.

MOODBOARDS — YOUR CREATIVE COMPASS

Before you create anything—website, logo, photoshoot—you need a moodboard.

A moodboard shows the *feeling* of your brand before it becomes a design.

Elements of an Effective Moodboard

- Color inspiration
- Typography examples
- Imagery references
- Textures and patterns
- Layout inspiration
- Brand personality words

Best Practices

- Start broad (40–50 images)
- Narrow to 12–18 strong visuals
- Explain WHY each image fits
- Update annually if your brand evolves

Moodboards prevent misunderstandings and keep designers aligned.

Templates — Consistency Made Easy

Templates save time while ensuring every piece of content still looks on-brand.

Essential Templates

- Social media templates
- Presentation templates
- Proposal templates
- One-pager templates
- Website page templates
- Email signature templates
- Business document templates

Templates should make branding easier—not harder.

Standard

Templates must be:

- Easy to customize
- Clean and modern
- Clearly branded
- Sized correctly
- Usable by non-designers

Templates are how your brand stays consistent at scale.

FINAL THOUGHT FOR THIS CHAPTER

Visual branding is not about over-designing or chasing trends.
It's about establishing recognizable patterns that create trust.

When your colors, typography, spacing, imagery, and templates all follow clear standards, your brand becomes unmistakable. And when your visuals align with your personality and messaging, your brand becomes unforgettable.

Visual standards aren't about beauty.
They're about clarity, consistency, and trust.

PART II – DIGITAL PRESENCE: THE MODERN BATTLEFIELD

WHAT ONLINE PRESENCE REALLY MEANS

Most people think "online presence" means having a website or being active on social media. But in today's digital world, your online presence is much bigger. It's every place your business shows up—intentionally or unintentionally. It's every touch-point, every mention, every search result, every review, every listing, and every interaction connected to your name.

Your online presence is what customers see **before** you speak.
It's what they judge **before** they buy.
It's what they believe **before** you have a chance to explain.

And that reality requires a level of clarity and consistency most brands were never taught to maintain.

WHAT COUNTS AS YOUR PRESENCE

Your online presence includes everything tied to your business—whether you created it or not. It's not one platform. It's the collection of all of them.

Here's what truly makes up your presence:

1. Your Website

Your digital home and your first impression.

It communicates:

- Professionalism
- Legitimacy
- What you do
- Who you serve
- How to work with you

A slow, outdated, or confusing website is an instant credibility killer.

2. Social Media Profiles

Active or not, they represent your brand.
Empty pages communicate neglect.
Inconsistent visuals communicate confusion.

3. Google Search Results

People look you up before contacting you.

They see:

- Reviews
- Mentions
- Articles
- Old listings
- Outdated pages
- Photos tied to your name

This is part of your presence—even if you didn't put it there.

4. Online Articles & Press Mentions

Anything written about you becomes part of your brand story—good or bad.

5. Customer Reviews

Reviews shape perception faster than your website does.
Not responding to reviews looks careless.

6. Business Listings

Google Business Profile, Yelp, Bing, Apple Maps, industry directories.

Your info must match everywhere—hours, address, phone.

7. Public Photos or Videos

Tagged photos, event footage, videos attached to your location—even if you
never approved them.

8. Emails & Client Communication

Your email tone, structure, signature, and professionalism all reflect your brand.

9. Online Ads

Even temporary campaigns influence how customers see you.

10. Digital Behavior

How you message.
How you respond.
How you show up publicly.
It all counts.

Your online presence is far larger than most business owners realize.

WHAT HARMS YOUR PRESENCE

Your presence can be weakened by things you control—and things you don't.

Understanding these risks helps you protect your reputation:

1. Inconsistent Branding

Different logos, colors, fonts, or messaging across platforms confuses customers.

2. Outdated Information

Old hours, wrong prices, unclear services, incorrect addresses—these break trust instantly.

3. Poor Website Performance

Slow load times, cluttered layouts, broken buttons, confusing navigation—people leave fast.

4. Neglected Social Media

A page that hasn't posted in years feels abandoned.

5. Bad Reviews Without Response

Silence communicates negligence.
Even a calm, professional reply can rebuild trust.

6. Unprofessional Content

Blurry graphics, mismatched colors, stretched logos, messy designs—all lower your authority.

7. Inconsistent Tone

If your website sounds polished but your emails sound sloppy, customers notice.

8. Trend-Chasing

Random aesthetics, random messaging, random posting styles—you lose identity.

9. Weak Mobile Experience

Most people browse on mobile.
If your site isn't mobile-friendly, your business feels outdated.

10. No Clear Call-to-Action

If customers don't know the next step, they leave.

Your presence isn't harmed only by what you publish.
It's harmed by what you **fail to maintain.**

HOW CUSTOMERS JUDGE YOU IN 3–7 SECONDS

Customers make decisions extremely quickly.

In the first **3 to 7 seconds**, they decide:

- Do I trust this business?
- Do they look professional?
- Do they feel current?
- Do I understand what they do?
- Do I feel safe buying from them?
- Does this brand feel like it's for me?

These judgments happen subconsciously and are based on:

Visual Clarity

Clean layout, spacing, colors, consistent elements.

Speed

A slow site loses visitors before anything loads.

Messaging Clarity

People must instantly understand what you do and why it matters.

Professional Appearance

Fonts, color palette, photo quality, formatting—all signal credibility.

Emotional Alignment

Your tone either connects or pushes someone away.

You don't get a second chance at a digital first impression.

DEVICE-FIRST MINDSET

Most people experience your brand through a device—especially their phone. That means your online presence must work seamlessly on small screens.

A device-first brand understands:

1. Mobile is Primary

Design for mobile first, then expand to desktop.
If it doesn't work on mobile, it doesn't work at all.

2. Speed Is More Important Than Aesthetics

Beautiful design won't matter if your site loads slowly.

3. Clarity Beats Creativity

Small screens demand simple, readable, skimmable layouts.

4. Touch-Friendly Navigation

Buttons must be easy to tap, menus must be easy to open, and forms must be easy to fill.

5. Shorter Text, Stronger Message

People skim on mobile.
Your message must hit quickly.

6. Every Platform Behaves Differently

Social media, websites, email newsletters, and online listings all display differently on mobile.

Modern customers expect effortless digital experiences.
They compare you to the world's biggest brands—not just your direct competitors.

A device-first mindset keeps you relevant, usable, and trustworthy.

FINAL THOUGHT FOR THIS CHAPTER

Online presence is not just about showing up.
It's about showing up **well, consistently,** and **intentionally** across every digital touchpoint.

When you understand:

- what actually counts,
- what harms your presence,
- how customers judge quickly, and
- how device-first behavior shapes decisions…

…you gain control of the narrative customers build about your brand.

A strong online presence doesn't happen by accident.
It happens by discipline, upkeep, and standards.

WEBSITE FOUNDATIONS:
THE NON-NEGOTIABLES

Your website is the center of your brand's online presence. Not your social media, not your directory listings, not your ads—your website. It's the digital property you fully own. It's your storefront, your introduction, your credibility check, and often the first encounter a customer has with your business before you ever speak a word.

A strong brand cannot exist online without a strong website.
And a weak website can undo years of hard work in seconds.

This chapter outlines the **non-negotiables**—the standards, requirements, and foundational principles every modern website must meet. These aren't "nice to have" features, and they aren't optional based on preference. They are the baseline for being considered professional, trustworthy, and worthy of your customer's time.

If your website doesn't meet these standards, everything else—your ads, content, social media, SEO—will work twice as hard for half the results.

Let's break down what every website must have.

STRUCTURE & NAVIGATION

Structure is how the site is built.
Navigation is how users move through it.
Together, they determine whether people stay or silently disappear.

Most users won't tell you your site is confusing—they'll just leave.

What Good Structure Looks Like

A well-organized website feels effortless to explore:

- Clear, predictable menu structure
- 5–7 main navigation items max
- Simple page titles (Home, About, Services, Contact)
- Logical hierarchy (H1 → H2 → H3)
- Footer that mirrors most primary links
- No clutter, no chaos
- Clear call-to-action on every page
- Content organized by user need—not internal company structure

Good navigation is invisible.
Users don't think about it because it works.

What Bad Structure Looks Like

- Too many menu options
- Clever labels that confuse ("Our Philosophy" instead of "About")
- Buried information
- Disorganized pages
- Missing CTAs
- A navigation that changes from page to page
- No clear order or logic

When users get lost, they leave.
When users hesitate, they leave.

Standard

Your website should answer three questions within seconds:

"Where am I?"
"What is this?"
"What do I do next?"

If users cannot answer those instantly—you have a structure problem.

SPEED & PERFORMANCE

Speed is trust.
If your site loads slowly, customers assume your business operates slowly.
They won't wait—they'll go somewhere else.

Speed Non-Negotiables

- Load time under **3 seconds** (under 2 seconds is ideal)
- Optimized images (compressed, correct format, sized properly)
- Clean code (minified CSS/JS, no bloat)
- Minimal plugins and third-party scripts
- CDN (Content Delivery Network) enabled
- Caching enabled
- Fast, reliable hosting
- No oversized videos or auto-play animations
- Lazy loading for images and embeds
- No layout shifts (CLS under 0.1)

Why Speed Is Critical

- Every additional second of load time = **7% fewer conversions**
- Google ranks fast sites higher
- Slow websites feel outdated, unsafe, and unprofessional

Common Mistake

Choosing visuals over performance.

A beautiful site that loads slowly is a broken site.

Standard

Speed beats style when style slows the site down.

ACCESSIBILITY

Accessibility is not optional.
It's a brand standard.
And it's the difference between being inclusive and being careless.

Accessibility ensures your website works for everyone—including users with vision impairments, mobility challenges, hearing disabilities, and neurodivergence.

Accessibility Includes:

- Readable, scalable font sizes (minimum 16px for body text)
- Proper color contrast (WCAG AA 4.5:1 or higher)
- Alt text for all meaningful images
- Clear headings and structure
- Keyboard-friendly navigation
- Visible focus states for links and buttons
- Clear, descriptive button/link labels ("View Pricing," not "Click Here")
- Captions or transcripts for videos
- Error messages that explain what to fix

WCAG Standards

Most brands should aim for **WCAG 2.1 Level AA**, which ensures:

- Readability
- Usability
- Keyboard accessibility
- Assistive technology compatibility
- Clear structure
- Proper spacing and labeling

Common Mistake

Designing something "pretty" that no one can actually use.

Standard

If someone with vision, hearing, cognitive, or mobility challenges cannot use your site, your design needs improvement.

Accessibility isn't just ethical—it improves SEO, usability, and overall user experience for everyone.

MOBILE EXPERIENCE

In today's world, mobile is the primary experience—not desktop.

More than 60% of website traffic arrives from phones. For many industries, it's over 75%. Your site must be **deliberately designed** for mobile screens—not shrunk from desktop layouts.

Mobile Non-Negotiables

- Clean, vertical layout
- Buttons large enough to tap (at least 44x44px)
- Menus that open smoothly
- Readable text without zoom
- Fast load times even on cellular
- Images that resize properly
- Zero horizontal scrolling
- CTAs easily reached with the thumb
- Forms simplified for small screens
- Reduced typing requirements
- Auto-fill enabled
- No intrusive pop-ups

Mobile Problems That Kill Trust

- Tiny text
- Impossible-to-tap links
- Images that bleed off the screen
- Menus that don't open
- Slow load times on LTE
- Forms that require too much typing

Common Mistake

Shrinking the desktop design down—rather than building mobile up.

Standard

Your website must feel designed for mobile, not squeezed into mobile.

SECURITY

Security is a silent trust factor.
Customers may never see it—but they will absolutely feel the lack of it.

A single breach, infected form, or hacked page can destroy trust permanently.

Security Non-Negotiables

- SSL certificate (HTTPS required)
- Updated plugins / themes / software
- Strong, unique passwords
- Two-factor authentication for admin accounts
- Daily automated backups stored off-site
- Malware scanning
- Web Application Firewall (WAF)
- Spam protection for forms
- Secure hosting platform
- No abandoned plugins or outdated dependencies

Common Mistake

Believing security is "only for big companies."

Hackers target small businesses because they assume security is weak.

Standard

A secure website protects:

- Your customers
- Your reputation
- Your brand integrity
- Your revenue

Security must be maintained—not assumed.

COPYWRITING STANDARDS

Words determine whether a user:

- Stays or leaves
- Trusts or doubts
- Understands or gets confused
- Takes action or clicks away

Copywriting is design.
Copywriting is UX.
Copywriting is branding.

Copywriting Non-Negotiables

Your website must clearly communicate:

- What you do
- Who you help
- How you help them
- Why you're the right choice
- What the next step is

This must be visible **above the fold** on your homepage.

Style Standards

- Short paragraphs (2–4 lines max)
- Clear, powerful headlines
- Benefit-focused language
- Simple, conversational tone
- Proof-based claims
- User-centered messaging
- Active voice
- Specific CTAs
- Avoiding jargon and vague language

Common Mistake

Writing paragraphs that sound good, but say nothing.

Example of bad writing:
"Empowering businesses through innovative digital solutions."

What does that even mean?

Standard

If someone has to re-read your content to understand it, simplify it.

USER BEHAVIOR PATTERNS

Websites fail when they're designed based on personal preference instead of human behavior.

People do not read websites—they scan them.
People do not explore—they look for the quickest path.
People do not guess—they bail.

Understanding behavior is non-negotiable.

How People Actually Use Websites

- They skim—headlines, bold text, buttons.
- They scroll before clicking anything.
- Their eyes go to the top-left first.
- They avoid clutter and confusion.
- They judge credibility instantly.
- They seek clarity, not creativity.
- They expect consistency across pages.
- They click clear CTAs.
- They abandon pages that feel overwhelming.

Heat Maps & Analytics Reveal Patterns

Tools like:

- Hotjar
- Microsoft Clarity
- Google Analytics
- Crazy Egg

…show where users click, scroll, hesitate, or abandon.

Common Mistake

Designing the site based on what the owner wants, not what the user needs.

Standard

Your website must reflect user psychology, not preference.

FINAL THOUGHT FOR THIS CHAPTER

A website isn't just *part* of your online presence—
it is your online presence.

It's where every ad, every post, every link, every mention, and every Google search leads back to. It's the core of your brand's digital ecosystem.

When your website follows these non-negotiables—
✓ clear structure
✓ fast speed
✓ full accessibility
✓ mobile-first design
✓ strong security
✓ clean, clear copywriting
✓ user-centered behavior

—your site becomes a tool that works for you 24/7. It sells when you're asleep. It builds trust before you speak. It communicates professionalism before the conversation begins.

These standards don't make your site pretty.
They make your site effective.
And effectiveness builds trust.

THE BRANDNAMESITES WEBSITE FRAMEWORK

A website is not a collection of pretty pages and random thoughts placed across a screen. It is a system. Every section, every button, every headline, and every pixel should work together to guide the visitor, communicate your value, build trust, and lead them toward the next step. A website that works feels intentional. A website that merely exists feels confusing.

The BrandNameSites Website Framework is the standard we use to ensure every website we build is clear, modern, aligned, and strategic. These are not suggestions. These are requirements for building a credible, conversion-focused online presence.

This chapter outlines the framework page by page so you always know exactly what a strong, professional website must include—from the homepage that makes your first impression to the contact page that closes the deal, and every structural component in between.

THE PHILOSOPHY BEHIND THE FRAMEWORK

Before diving into the page-by-page breakdown, it's important to understand the thinking behind the framework itself. Everything we build at BrandNameSites rests on three core principles:

1. Clarity Over Cleverness

Visitors don't want to decode your message. They want to understand it instantly.

Bad example:
"We architect digital experiences that catalyze transformative outcomes."

Good example:
"We build websites that turn visitors into customers."

The rule:
If a seventh grader can't understand what you do, it's too complicated.

2. Conversion-Focused Design

Every element should have a purpose. If it doesn't guide users toward action, it's decoration.

Ask these questions about every page element:

- Does this build trust?
- Does this answer a question?
- Does this remove friction?
- Does this lead users closer to a decision?

If the answer is no—remove it.

3. Brand Consistency at Scale

Your website should feel like *your brand*, not a template with your logo slapped on.

That means:

- Same tone and voice across all pages
- Same visual identity (colors, spacing, typography)
- Same structure and flow
- Same personality
- Same quality everywhere

Brand consistency is one of the strongest subconscious trust signals in digital design.

1. HOMEPAGE REQUIREMENTS

Your homepage is your digital first impression. It must answer these three questions within seconds:

1. **Who are you?**
2. **What do you do?**
3. **Who do you do it for?**

If someone can't answer these by simply glancing at your homepage, the homepage is not doing its job.

The homepage is also your front door, your handshake, your positioning, and the immediate moment where a visitor decides whether your brand feels trustworthy, confusing, or forgettable.

THE STANDARD HOMEPAGE SECTIONS

Below is the BrandNameSites homepage structure—a proven sequence that creates clarity, builds trust, guides decision-making, and improves conversions.

1. Navigation & Header

Must include:

- Logo (top left, always clickable)
- Clear navigation (5–7 main items max)
- Optional support link or search
- Mobile hamburger menu
- Consistent placement across all pages

2. Hero Section (The Most Important Section)

Required elements:

1. **Clear headline (H1)**
   - Your core value in 8–12 words
   - Not clever, just clear
2. **Subheadline**
   - Clarifies the headline
   - 15–25 words
   - A simple explanation of what you do and who you help
3. **Primary Call-to-Action Button**
   Examples:
   - "Get Started"
   - "Book a Call"
   - "Request a Quote"

   Must be bold, high contrast, tap-friendly on mobile.
4. **Hero Image or Video**
   - Professional quality
   - Represents your work or your audience
   - Must not slow the page down
5. **Optional Trust Signal**
   - "Trusted by 200+ businesses"
   - Client logos
   - Certifications or awards

Common Mistake:
"Welcome to our website!" is not a headline. It's wasted space.

3. Quick Value Statement

A short, confident line that explains your big benefit.

Examples:

- "Professional websites built for speed, clarity, and conversion."
- "Brand-first design that turns visitors into customers."

This helps anchor your identity.

4. Problem/Solution Block

Show empathy. Then show your solution.

Customers should feel understood.

Your problem examples:

- Your website looks outdated
- Your site is slow
- You're losing customers to competitors
- DIY templates aren't converting

Your solution example:
"We build fast, modern, conversion-focused websites that reflect your brand and deliver results."

5. Services Snapshot

A clean 3–5 block overview of what you offer.

Each service block includes:

- Icon or small image
- Simple service name
- 1–2 sentence description
- Link to full page

Rule:
Each service block must be scannable in under 5 seconds.

6. How It Works (Your Process)

People fear the unknown. Showing your process removes anxiety.

The standard is a simple 3–5 step flow:

1. Discovery call
2. Strategy and design
3. Build and test
4. Launch and support

Each step includes an icon, a short description, and a clear, calm tone.

7. Social Proof Section

You must show proof before you ask for action.

Social proof options:

- Testimonials
- Case studies
- Real client photos
- Quick results
- Ratings
- "Trusted by" logos

Specificity builds trust.
"Working with them was great" is not enough.

8. Why Choose Us (Differentiators)

Explain what makes you different.

Examples:

- No templates—ever
- You own your website 100%
- Built for speed
- Ongoing support
- Transparent pricing

Use 3–4 strong differentiators. No fluff.

9. Final Call-to-Action

Close the page with a direct, encouraging CTA.

Examples:

- "Ready to build a website that actually works?"
- "Book your free strategy call."

For visitors not ready yet, include a softer secondary option.

Homepage Warning

If your homepage feels cluttered or confusing, customers leave instantly.

Clarity is a non-negotiable.

2. SERVICES LAYOUT STANDARD

People don't want to guess what you offer. They want clarity, simplicity, and a clear next step.

Each service page must communicate your service in under 45 seconds.

SERVICE PAGE REQUIREMENTS

1. Clear Service Title

Say what it is—not what you call it internally.

Examples:

- "Website Design"
- "Brand Identity Development"
- "Social Media Strategy"

2. Short Introduction

Two sentences that describe what you offer and who it's for.

3. Benefits-First Breakdown

People buy outcomes, not features.

Example:

- Faster website = more conversions
- Clear branding = stronger audience connection
- Better structure = improved user experience

Lead with benefits, not features.

4. What's Included

A simple bullet list. No essays.

5. Process or Steps

Demystify the workflow. Remove fear. Increase trust.

6. Pricing Structure

Transparent, organized, easy to understand.

If you don't want to list full pricing, use:

- "Starting at $_____"
- "Custom to your project size"

7. Testimonials or Proof

Social proof tied to this specific service.

8. Strong Call-to-Action

Direct, simple, and intentional.

Optional: Comparison Table

For multi-tier pricing, use a comparison grid.

This works extremely well for agencies.

Warning

Too much text confuses.
Too little text leaves doubt.

Write for clarity.

3. ABOUT PAGE STRUCTURE

Your About page is not your autobiography.
It's your credibility page.

The visitor is not asking for your life story.
They're asking:

- Can I trust you?
- Do you understand my needs?
- Are you qualified?

Here is the structure that answers those questions clearly.

ABOUT PAGE REQUIREMENTS

1. Who You Are

Short, simple introduction of you or your team.

2. What You Believe

List 3–5 brand values or principles.

3. Why You Exist

Your brand purpose, written in simple, human language.

4. Your Story (Short Version)

Only include the parts relevant to your brand and your impact.

5. Your Approach

How you work and what clients can expect.

6. Visuals

Professional photo or brand-aligned graphics.

Humans trust humans.

7. Call-to-Action

"Let's work together."
"Book a discovery call."

Warning:

People want connection—not a timeline.
Keep it intentional.

4. CONTACT & CONVERSION STANDARDS

Your contact page is not decoration. It is a conversion tool.

CONTACT PAGE REQUIREMENTS

1. Simple Contact Form

Name, email, message.

Optional: phone, business name, timeline.

Every extra field reduces submissions by ~10%.

2. Clear Call-to-Action

Tell them exactly what will happen.

"Submit" is not a CTA.
"Request a Consultation" is.

3. Response Expectations

Set expectations:

"We respond within 24 hours."

4. Email + Phone (optional)

Professional and separate from personal.

5. Reassurance Statement

"Your information is safe. We never share your data."

Conversion Standards

Conversion happens when:

- The next step is clear
- The user feels informed
- The form is simple
- Trust is visible

Warning:
If your contact page looks abandoned, people assume your business is too.

5. GLOBAL BRANDING CONSISTENCY

Every part of your site must feel like it belongs to one brand.

This includes:

- Colors
- Typography
- Spacing
- Icons
- Layout
- Voice
- Tone
- Buttons
- Imagery style

Consistency builds trust. Inconsistency destroys it.

Global Standards

Your website must use:

- One color style
- One typography system
- One voice and tone
- One spacing structure
- One style of imagery
- One button style

If every page looks like a different designer built it, your brand loses authority.

6. UI/UX BEST PRACTICES

UI (what users see)
UX (how users feel while using it)

This is where clarity meets functionality.

UI/UX Standards

1. Simple Layouts

Clarity beats creativity every time.

2. Predictable Navigation

Users should know exactly where they are.

3. Strong Visual Hierarchy

Headlines large. Paragraphs small. Buttons noticeable.

4. Buttons That Stand Out

Consistent action color.

5. Ample White Space

Space creates professionalism.

6. High Readability

Short sentences. Short paragraphs. Simple words.

7. Minimal Pop-Ups

Use only when necessary.

8. No Scroll Jams

Nothing should interrupt scrolling.

9. Smooth Animations

Subtle, purposeful, not distracting.

10. Meaningful Visuals

Images used for clarity, not decoration.

Warning:

Bad UX doesn't always look bad.
It *feels* bad.
And when something feels bad, users quietly leave.

7. SEO & AEO MINIMUMS

Your website must be found by both humans and AI systems.

SEO Essentials

- Keyword clarity
- On-page optimization
- Proper title tags and meta descriptions
- Structured content
- Alt text
- Internal linking
- Clean URL structure
- Mobile-first performance
- Strong E-E-A-T (Experience, Expertise, Authoritativeness, Trustworthiness)

AEO Essentials

AI systems prefer content that is:

- Clear
- Question-and-answer structured
- Organized
- Supported by schema markup
- Easy to summarize

FAQs, lists, and direct answers increase your visibility in AI search tools.

8. WEBSITE ECOSYSTEM CHART

Your website is the hub of your digital ecosystem. Everything—social media, email, ads, SEO, partnerships—flows back to it.

The ecosystem must be mapped so every page has purpose.

A strong ecosystem includes:

- Homepage
- Services
- About
- Portfolio
- Contact
- Blog
- FAQ
- Legal pages
- Optional support pages

Mapping your pages ensures no page is orphaned and every user path is logical.

9. THE BRANDNAMESITES SIGNATURE WEBSITE ANATOMY

This is the complete structure we recommend for all high-performing websites:

- Sticky header
- Clear hero
- Trust indicators
- Problem → solution
- Process
- Services
- Social proof
- Differentiators
- Final CTA
- Clean footer

It is simple.
It is strategic.
It is effective.

FINAL THOUGHT FOR THIS CHAPTER

The BrandNameSites Website Framework gives structure, clarity, and direction. When every page follows the same standards, your website becomes:

- Organized
- Trustworthy
- Consistent
- Scannable
- User-friendly
- Conversion-focused

A strong website is not built from inspiration.
It is built from **standards**.

PART III – CONTENT SYSTEMS FOR BRAND

CONTENT IDENTITY VS CONTENT STRATEGY

Content is one of the most powerful tools in modern branding—but also one of the most misunderstood. Many businesses struggle with content not because they lack ideas, but because they lack clarity on who they are online and how they should show up.

Content is not just what you post.
Content is how your brand communicates with the world.

This chapter breaks down the two pillars of digital communication—**content identity** and **content strategy**. These terms are often used interchangeably, but they serve very different roles. When you understand both, and how they work together, your content becomes clear, consistent, recognizable, and trusted.

THE DIFFERENCE: CONTENT IDENTITY VS. CONTENT STRATEGY

You cannot create powerful content without understanding two things:

Who you are in your content (Identity)
How you show up through your content (Strategy)

Most brands create content backwards. They start posting because "you're supposed to." They write blogs because "it helps SEO." They film videos because "everyone is doing it."

But without identity and strategy, content becomes random, inconsistent, and forgettable.

This chapter fixes that.

CONTENT IDENTITY — Who You Are When You Communicate

Content identity is the personality, voice, tone, values, and perspective your brand expresses in everything you publish.

It answers the deeper identity questions:

- What do we consistently talk about?
- How do we sound?
- What do we believe?
- How do we treat our audience?
- What topics fit our brand—and what topics do not?
- What makes our content recognizable?

Content identity is the DNA of your content. Someone should be able to read a post, watch a video, or listen to a message and say:

"This sounds like them."

WHAT CONTENT IDENTITY INCLUDES

1. Voice & Tone

Your voice is your personality in words; your tone adjusts based on context.

A branded voice is:

- Consistent across all platforms
- Recognizable without the logo
- An extension of your brand personality
- Adaptable (educational vs. promotional vs. supportive)

Example of a consistent voice:

- Blog: Conversational but informative
- Social: Quick, casual, engaging
- Email: Personal, direct, helpful
- Video: Friendly, confident, approachable

2. Visual Identity in Content

Your content also has a *look*, not just a voice.

This includes:

- Color and typography
- Photography style (moody, bright, candid, polished)
- Graphic templates
- Iconography
- Video style and editing rhythm
- Filters, overlays, framing

If someone can see your content without seeing your logo and still know it's yours—you have strong visual identity.

3. Topic Authority (What You Talk About)

Your identity defines what is "in scope" and what is not.

Example: A financial brand might talk about:

- Personal finance
- Investing basics
- Debt reduction
- Money mindset

But *not*:

- Day trading
- Corporate finance
- Cryptocurrency speculation
- Political commentary

Your identity determines what belongs to you—and what doesn't.

4. Content Themes (Pillars)

These are the recurring themes your brand returns to over and over.

For a web design agency, themes might include:

1. Website performance (speed, optimization)
2. User experience and conversion
3. Branding and identity
4. Content strategy
5. Avoiding DIY website mistakes

Themes create cohesion. Random posting destroys trust.

5. Point of View (POV)

Your point of view is your unique stance or "truth" in your industry.

Ask yourself:

- What do we believe that others don't?
- What frustrates us about the industry?
- What truths do we speak that others avoid?
- What do we champion that's undervalued?

Example POV:
"Most websites are built for designers—not customers."

Point-of-view content makes you memorable.
A brand without a POV becomes generic and interchangeable.

CONTENT STRATEGY — How You Show Up

If content identity makes the content *feel* like you, content strategy makes the content *work* for you.

Content strategy is the intentional plan behind your content:

- What you create
- Why you create it
- Where you publish it
- When you publish it
- Who it serves
- What it is supposed to do

This is where consistency, planning, goals, and execution meet.

WHAT CONTENT STRATEGY INCLUDES

1. Goals

You must define *why* you're creating content.

Common content goals:

- Brand awareness
- Lead generation
- Customer education
- Authority building
- Retention
- Traffic & search ranking
- Community engagement

Every piece of content must connect to a purpose.
If it doesn't, don't create it.

2. Audience

You're not creating content for "everyone."
Different audiences need different kinds of content.

Example: A business coach might segment:

- New entrepreneurs
- Established small business owners
- Former corporate employees
- Creatives starting freelance work

Each segment requires different language and topics.

3. Content Types

Written:

- Blogs
- Captions
- Emails
- Guides
- Case studies

Visual:

- Graphics
- Infographics
- Photography
- Carousels

Video:

- Reels
- YouTube
- Tutorials
- Testimonials
- Webinars

Audio:

- Podcasts
- Voice notes
- Audio summaries

Choose formats you can sustain.
Don't try everything and master nothing.

4. Distribution Channels

Owned channels:

- Website
- Blog
- Email
- Podcast
- YouTube

Rented channels:

- Instagram
- TikTok
- Facebook
- LinkedIn
- Twitter/X

Earned channels:

- Guest features
- Press
- Collaborations
- Referrals
- User-generated content

Rule: **Rented channels grow your audience. Owned channels convert your audience.**

5. Content Calendar

Consistency matters more than volume.

General guidelines:

- Blog: 1–4 posts/month
- Email: 1–4x/month
- Instagram/TikTok: 3–7x/week
- LinkedIn: 2–5x/week
- YouTube: 1–4x/month

The rule: **Show up consistently. Not constantly.**

HOW IDENTITY & STRATEGY WORK TOGETHER

Example: A fitness coach:

Identity

- Voice: Motivational but grounded
- Visual: Real bodies, natural lighting
- Themes: Strength > aesthetics, mental health
- POV: "Fitness is about feeling strong, not looking perfect."

Strategy

- Goal: Lead generation for 12-week program
- Audience: Busy professionals
- Content types: Reels, blog posts, emails
- Distribution: Instagram → Website → Email funnel
- Calendar: 5 reels/week, 1 email/week

Identity = recognizable
Strategy = effective
Together = powerful

THE ROLE OF CONTENT IN TRUST

Content is the bridge between "never heard of you" and "ready to buy."

Content builds trust by being:

- Clear
- Helpful
- Consistent
- Relevant
- Professional
- Authentic
- Aligned

Content damages trust when it is:

- Random
- Inconsistent
- Confusing
- Off-brand
- Outdated
- Poor quality
- Imitative instead of original

People don't trust brands that post once in a while.
People trust brands that show up consistently with clarity and value.

CONTENT TYPES & WHEN TO USE THEM

1. Educational Content

Purpose: Teach, simplify, empower
Examples:

- How-to posts
- Tutorials
- Step-by-step guides
- Industry insights
- Checklists

2. Value-Based Content

Purpose: Show beliefs & values
Examples:

- What you stand for
- Opinions
- Lessons learned
- Why your process matters

3. Story-Based Content

Purpose: Build connection
Examples:

- Origin stories
- Client moments
- Behind the scenes
- Transformations

4. Promotional Content

Purpose: Drive sales or conversions
Examples:

- Launch announcements
- Limited offers
- Service promotions
- Case studies
- Testimonials

5. Engagement Content

Purpose: Encourage interaction
Examples:

- Polls
- Questions
- Relatable posts

6. Social Proof Content

Purpose: Build credibility
Examples:

- Testimonials
- Reviews
- Case studies
- User-generated content

7. Long-Form Content

Purpose: Establish expertise
Examples:

- Articles
- Ebooks
- Webinars
- Deep-dive videos

8. Website Content

Purpose: Build long-term trust
Examples:

- Landing pages
- Resource pages
- SEO articles
- Product descriptions

THE CUSTOMER JOURNEY & CONTENT

Stage 1: Awareness

Goal: "Who are you?"
Content: Educational, inspirational, scroll-stoppers

Stage 2: Interest

Goal: "Why should I listen?"
Content: Guides, insights, how-tos

Stage 3: Consideration

Goal: "Why should I trust you?"
Content: Testimonials, case studies, FAQs

Stage 4: Conversion

Goal: "Why should I buy now?"
Content: Sales pages, offers, strong CTAs

Stage 5: Retention

Goal: "Why should I stay?"
Content: Tutorials, updates, community content

If your content doesn't support all stages, your brand will struggle with conversions.

CONTENT PILLARS: THE FRAMEWORK OF CONSISTENCY

You need 3–5 core pillars (themes) your brand consistently speaks about.

Why pillars matter:

- Reduce randomness
- Increase authority
- Improve focus
- Make content planning easier

Example for a web agency:

1. Website design & branding
2. Performance & technical standards
3. User experience & conversion
4. SEO & content strategy
5. Common mistakes to avoid

Rotate through your pillars weekly to stay balanced.

BALANCING CONTENT TYPES: THE 80/20 RULE

80% Value
20% Promotion

This ratio builds trust while still generating sales.

Weekly example:

- Mon: Educational post
- Tue: Client story
- Wed: Tip or breakdown
- Thu: Social proof
- Fri: Promotion (CTA)

4 value posts, 1 promotional.

CONTENT REPURPOSING: CREATE ONCE, DISTRIBUTE EVERYWHERE

One long-form content piece can become:

- 3–5 social posts
- 1 newsletter
- 1 LinkedIn article
- 5–10 quote graphics
- Multiple short videos
- Story content
- Blog excerpts

This multiplies your impact without burning out.

MEASURING CONTENT SUCCESS

Measure based on your goals.

Awareness

- Reach
- Traffic
- Shares

Engagement

- Likes
- Comments
- Watch time

Lead Generation

- Email signups
- Downloads
- Form submissions

Conversions

- Sales
- Bookings
- Revenue-influenced

Avoid Vanity Metrics

Followers don't equal buyers.
Likes don't equal revenue.
Views don't equal trust.

Focus on what moves the business.

STANDARD

Every piece of content should reflect your:

- Brand voice
- Visual identity
- Purpose
- Audience
- Values
- Expertise

Anything else is noise.

COMMON MISTAKE

Posting because you "need to be active."

Correct:
Content should never be random.
Content should be intentional, aligned, and built from standards.

FINAL THOUGHT FOR THIS CHAPTER

Content identity shows your personality.
Content strategy organizes your presence.

Together, they create clarity, trust, and recognition.

When your content consistently reflects **who you are**—and shows up in a structured way—your brand becomes easier to recognize, easier to trust, and easier to choose.

Your content is not just information.
It is part of your identity.

SOCIAL MEDIA PRESENCE STANDARDS

Social media is not your brand—it is simply one expression of it. It's a storefront window, not the entire building. The problem for most businesses is not that they're "bad at social media," but that they are using it without clarity, structure, or standards. They show up everywhere with no intentional plan, or they disappear for weeks and resurface with randomness.

The truth is simple:
Social media should support your brand, not drain it.

This chapter outlines the BrandNameSites social media standards so your presence stays consistent, aligned, and professional—never trendy for the sake of trend, never overwhelming, never random. When used correctly, social media amplifies your credibility. When used incorrectly, it confuses your audience and weakens your identity.

To win online, you must understand what each platform is for, what it's not for, how to show up correctly, and how to ensure everything you post reflects your brand's identity and purpose.

THE PHILOSOPHY OF SOCIAL MEDIA

Before anything else, understand this:

Social Media Is Discovery, Not Destination.

The purpose of social media is to get people *to your website*—the place you own. On social platforms, you don't own your followers, you don't control the algorithm, and you can be restricted or shadow-banned without warning.

Think of this relationship like a highway:

Social media = billboards
Your website = the actual store

Your job is to use social platforms to attract, interest, and direct people toward the space where conversions happen.

You don't need to be everywhere.
You need to be where your audience is—and you need to do it well.

WHAT TO USE EACH PLATFORM FOR

Each platform has strengths. When you use them for what they were designed for, your presence becomes easier, more intentional, and more effective.

Facebook

Best for:

- Community building
- Groups
- Event promotion
- Customer conversation
- Long-form insights
- Local engagement

Why it works:
Facebook supports relationship-building and deeper, conversational communication.

Don't use Facebook for:

- Posting personal drama
- Arguing publicly
- One-way sales blasting
- Neglecting comments or messages
- Letting information go outdated

Organic reach declines on Facebook unless your content is purposeful, helpful, or community-driven.

Instagram

Best for:

- Visual storytelling
- Reels
- Lifestyle or brand personality
- Behind-the-scenes
- Testimonials
- Portfolio-style showcasing

Why it works:
Instagram rewards aesthetic cohesion, storytelling, and short-form value.

Don't use Instagram for:

- Unbranded visuals
- Random aesthetics
- Trend-chasing without purpose
- Poor-quality media
- Long educational text without visuals

Instagram is a visual magazine—your grid is a design asset.

TikTok

Best for:

- Fast educational tips
- Relatable personality content
- Simplified breakdowns
- Trend-influenced short videos

Why it works:
TikTok favors authenticity and speed—quick, useful, human content over perfection.

Don't use TikTok for:

- Overly polished videos
- Hard selling
- Content that lacks a face or personality
- Forced trends that don't match your brand

TikTok is a place where being human matters more than being pretty.

LinkedIn

Best for:

- Professional credibility
- Thought leadership
- Industry insights
- Company updates
- Case studies
- B2B networking

Why it works:
LinkedIn rewards expertise, clarity, and depth.

Don't use LinkedIn for:

- Personal oversharing
- Emotional rants
- Off-topic posts
- Robotic corporate language
- Clickbait without substance

People come here for value and intelligence—respect the audience.

YouTube

Best for:

- Tutorials
- In-depth education
- Evergreen lessons
- Product walkthroughs
- Thought leadership

Why it works:
YouTube is a search engine, not just a social platform—your content lives for years.

Don't use YouTube for:

- Poor audio or video
- Long intros
- Aimless rambling
- Abandoning your comment section

A strong YouTube channel becomes a knowledge asset for your business.

Pinterest

Best for:

- Idea discovery
- Mood boards
- Inspiration
- Driving traffic to your blog or website

Why it works:
Pinterest posts have long lifespans and support visual discoveries.

Don't use Pinterest for:

- Off-brand images
- Random pins
- Cluttered boards with no theme

Pinterest is visual organization—not randomness.

Twitter / X

Best for:

- Short insights
- Industry commentary
- Quick communication
- Developing a strong brand voice
- Real-time responses

Don't use Twitter/X for:

- Emotional reactions
- Arguments
- Spam
- Corporate stiffness

Brevity and clarity win here.

Google Business Profile

Best for:

- Local visibility
- Reviews
- Photos
- Updates
- SEO impact

Don't use it for:

- Outdated hours or location info
- Ignored reviews
- Unprofessional images

A polished Google profile influences purchasing decisions more than most realize.

Your Website (Yes, this is a social presence)

Your website is the **central hub**.
Every platform should point back to it.

Your website holds:

- SEO
- Long-form content
- Authority
- Trust signals
- Conversion actions

If your website is weak, your social content effectiveness drops dramatically.

WHAT NOT TO USE PLATFORMS FOR

Each platform has limitations. Misusing them can make your brand look confused, unprofessional, or scattered.

Avoid across all platforms:

- Emotional rants
- Off-brand humor
- Trend chasing
- Posting to "stay active"
- Aggressive selling
- Ignoring comments
- Outdated information
- Off-topic content

Consistency > volume.
Clarity > trends.
Professionalism > popularity.

POSTING STANDARDS

Consistency beats frequency.
Quality beats quantity.

General Posting Standards

- Show up consistently (even weekly is better than sporadically)
- Use brand colors, fonts, and layout
- Keep visuals clean and simple
- Prioritize high-quality photos and videos
- Keep captions focused and intentional
- Add a CTA when appropriate
- Avoid clutter
- Maintain your message architecture

If your content doesn't align with your brand, it doesn't belong on your feed.

VISUAL STANDARDS

Brand visuals must be consistent across all platforms. This builds recognition and trust.

Your visuals must include:

- One color palette
- Cohesive typography
- 1–2 layout systems
- Consistent editing style
- Templates for graphics
- Photos and videos that look intentional

If your feed looks like multiple people designed it with multiple moods, your brand loses credibility.

CONTENT STANDARDS

Every social post should educate, inspire, connect, or convert.

Avoid:

- Walls of text
- Over-explanations
- Aimless storytelling
- Posting without purpose
- Low-quality visuals
- Randomness

Everything must reflect your brand identity:

- Purpose
- Vision
- Values
- Signature language
- Audience
- Personality

If it's off-brand—it's off the table.

COPY STANDARDS

Your words represent your brand as much as your visuals do.

Your copy must be:

- Clear
- Concise
- Conversational but professional
- Helpful
- Benefit-driven
- On-brand in tone

Avoid:

- Corporate jargon
- Trendy slang that doesn't match your identity
- Long, confusing paragraphs
- Hard-selling
- Over-promising
- Emotional posting

A Strong Copy Formula

1. **Hook** — Grab attention in one line
2. **Message** — Say the essential idea clearly
3. **Takeaway** — Give value
4. **Call-to-action** (optional) — Tell them what to do next

This formula works on all platforms.

ENGAGEMENT STANDARDS

Engagement isn't just likes—it's how you show up in the conversation.

Good engagement is:

- Prompt
- Respectful
- Helpful
- Human
- Consistent
- On-brand

Engagement guidelines:

- Respond within 24–48 hours
- Never argue publicly
- Redirect conflict privately
- Thank positive commenters
- Be human, not robotic
- Keep responses short and friendly
- Encourage conversation

Ignoring your audience sends the message:
"We don't care."

WHAT BUILDS STRONG ENGAGEMENT

- Asking thoughtful questions
- Posting relatable content
- Staying consistent
- Sharing stories
- Responding quickly
- Showing personality within your standards

WHAT DAMAGES ENGAGEMENT

- Posting inconsistently
- Ignoring followers
- Emotional posting
- Trend-chasing
- Overly corporate language
- Failing to respond
- Poor-quality visuals or sound

Social media is a two-way street.
If you only broadcast and never engage, your presence becomes flat and forgettable.

THE SOCIAL MEDIA CONTENT CALENDAR (BNS STANDARD)

You need structure.

A simple weekly standard could be:

Plan weekly.
Create monthly.
Schedule consistently.

FINAL THOUGHT FOR THIS CHAPTER

Social media is not about posting every day.
It's not about chasing trends or hacks.
It's about clarity, consistency, and alignment.

When your social media presence:

- **Looks like your brand**
- **Sounds like your brand**
- **Feels like your brand**

…your audience begins to recognize you, trust you, and choose you.

Recognition builds trust.
Trust builds business.
Business builds longevity.

Social media becomes powerful only when it is consistent, intentional, and aligned with the identity you've built.

STORYTELLING AUTHORITY & BRAND POSITIONING

Branding is more than visuals, identity, or content—it's perception. It's the space your business occupies in the minds of your audience and how they interpret your presence online and offline. Storytelling shapes that perception. Authority protects it. Positioning defines it. Together, these elements determine whether your business becomes memorable or fades into the noise.

Modern branding is not about looking good—it's about standing for something, communicating it clearly, and showing up as a leader in your industry with consistency, conviction, and credibility. This chapter teaches you exactly how to position your brand, create emotional connection through storytelling, and build authority that lasts.

HOW TO POSITION YOURSELF

Positioning is how you place your brand in the market and in your customer's mind. It answers the foundational question:

"Why should a customer choose us instead of someone else?"

Strong positioning is:

- Clear
- Confident
- Simple
- Direct
- Consistent

It doesn't shift with trends. It doesn't try to appeal to everyone. It is anchored in who you are, who you serve, and what makes you different.

THE FOUR CORE ELEMENTS OF POSITIONING

1. **What You Offer**
   The value, service, or solution you provide.
2. **Who You Serve**
   Your defined audience—not "everyone." Specificity builds strength.
3. **How You Deliver It**
   Your process, standards, and approach.
4. **Why You're Different**
   Your method, philosophy, experience, or differentiator.

When these four elements are clear, your brand becomes unmistakable.

STRONG POSITIONING VS. WEAK POSITIONING

Strong positioning sounds like:

- "We build fast, strategic websites for small businesses who need clarity and conversion."
- "We help entrepreneurs communicate their brand with structure and simplicity."
- "We combine branding, structure, and design—not just visuals."

Weak positioning sounds like:

- "We make websites."
- "We do everything."
- "We help anyone with anything."

Rule:
The clearer your position, the stronger your brand becomes.

THE POSITIONING STATEMENT TEMPLATE

(Adapted from Version 3 — now aligned with Version 1)

Fill in the blanks:

For [target audience]
who [problem or need],
our [product/service]
is [category]
that [unique benefit].
Unlike [competitors],
we [key differentiator].

Example for BrandNameSites:
For small business owners
who feel overwhelmed by slow, inconsistent websites,
our strategic web and branding service
is a clarity-driven design solution
that builds websites fast, clean, and aligned with your identity.
Unlike template builders and corporate agencies,
we combine brand strategy and web structure at an accessible level.

Precise. Practical. Memorable.

YOUR PLACE IN THE MARKET

Your brand does not need to dominate the entire industry.
It only needs to **own one space: your lane.**

You don't compete with every business—you compete with those offering similar results to the same audience.

Your goal is to be:

- The clearest
- The most consistent
- The most trustworthy
- The most aligned with your audience's needs

You don't need the biggest audience.
You need the **right** audience.

THE FOUR TYPES OF POSITIONING

(From Version 3, integrated with Version 1)

1. Price Positioning

You're either budget or premium. You cannot be both.

2. Quality Positioning

You emphasize exceptional results and craftsmanship.

3. Niche Positioning

You specialize: industry, audience, or specific problem.

4. Challenger Positioning

You position against what's broken in your industry.

People love disruptors and underdogs.

WHAT MAKES YOU DIFFERENT

(Competitive Differentiation)

Differentiate through:

1. **Your process**
2. **Your values**
3. **Your delivery**
4. **Your guarantees**

5. **Your experience with clients**

When you articulate these well, your audience stops comparing you.

THE POWER OF STORYTELLING

Facts tell.
Stories sell.

People forget information but remember emotions. Stories create emotional connection, build trust, and communicate values naturally.

Every brand needs to master storytelling because:

- Stories are memorable
- Stories humanize your brand
- Stories explain your mission
- Stories show—not tell—your values
- Stories demonstrate impact
- Stories inspire action

A brand without stories feels flat. A brand with stories becomes unforgettable.

THE THREE STORIES EVERY BRAND MUST HAVE

1. Your Origin Story (Why You Started)

Show your humanity, your motivation, your catalyst moment.

Structure:

- The Before
- The Catalyst
- The Struggle
- The Breakthrough
- The Mission

2. Customer Transformation Story (Before/After)

Demonstrate real impact through real results.

Structure:

- Their struggle
- Why they chose you
- The process
- The results
- The long-term impact

3. Values Story (What You Stand For)

Values are proven in action—not listed on your website.

Structure:

- The situation
- The choice
- The cost
- The principle
- The lesson

These stories create depth, relatability, and trust.

STORYTELLING FRAMEWORKS

(Blending Version 1 simplicity with Version 3 depth)

1. Hero's Journey

For long-form, case studies, origin stories.

2. PAS — Problem, Agitate, Solve

For sales content and social media.

3. BAB — Before, After, Bridge

For short-form content and landing pages.

4. ABT — And, But, Therefore

For presentations and clear explanations.

Different stories require different structures—leaders know how to choose the right one.

HOW TO SOUND LIKE A LEADER

Leadership is not about shouting. It's about clarity, calm confidence, and conviction.

A leader's voice sounds like:

- Clear, not complicated
- Confident, not aggressive
- Direct, not harsh
- Helpful, not desperate
- Instructive, not preachy
- Consistent, not scattered

How to Sound Like a Leader

1. **Speak in solutions.**
   No fluff. No vagueness.
2. **Remove filler language.**
   Drop "maybe," "kinda," "hopefully."
3. **Teach calmly.**
   Guidance shows authority without intimidation.
4. **Use your signature language.**
   Repetition builds recognition.
5. **Stay consistent everywhere.**
   Your tone = your identity.

Test:
If your content sounds unsure, your audience will feel unsure.
If your tone is confident, your audience feels safe choosing you.

WHAT ELEVATES A BRAND BEYOND VISUALS

Visuals attract attention.
Depth keeps it.

An elevated brand has:

1. Clarity

People know who you are and what you stand for.

2. Consistency

Your visuals, voice, and message align everywhere.

3. Character

Your values, standards, and behavior show integrity.

4. Storytelling

Your mission and purpose are communicated clearly.

5. Expertise

You simplify complex topics and lead with insight.

6. Experience

Your process is smooth, structured, and predictable.

7. Discipline

You don't chase every trend—you move with intention.

8. Emotional Connection

Your audience feels seen and supported.

9. Standards

You uphold rules that protect your identity.

10. Leadership

Your brand feels confident, grounded, and trustworthy.

Pretty brands get attention.
Strong brands keep attention.
Elevated brands build loyalty and authority.

MARKET POSITIONING EXERCISES

1. The Competitor Audit

Identify strengths, weaknesses, and gaps.

2. "Unlike" Statement

"Unlike ___, we ___ because ___."

3. The "We Believe" Manifesto

Write 5–10 statements that shape your brand philosophy.

These exercises formalize your leadership and identity.

FINAL THOUGHT FOR THIS CHAPTER

Storytelling shapes how people understand you.
Authority shapes how people trust you.
Positioning shapes how people choose you.

When your brand is:

- Clear in voice
- Strong in message
- Consistent in behavior
- Confident in leadership

...you stop being "one of many" and become the brand people remember, respect, and prefer.

This is how brands rise beyond visuals and become leaders in their industry.

BUILT ON STANDARDS.

PART IV – THE ONLINE BRAND ECOSYSTEM

THE WEBSITE AS THE CENTER OF THE UNIVERSE

Most brands treat their website like a box to check. Something they "have to have." A digital placeholder. A link in a bio. A business requirement. But in reality, your website is not just a component of your brand—it is the *center* of your entire digital universe. It is the only place online where you have full control, full ownership, and full authority over how your brand is perceived.

Social media introduces you.
Your website decides whether anyone takes you seriously.

Everything—*every* platform, *every* piece of content, *every* audience touchpoint—ultimately leads back to one destination: your website. No matter where people discover you first, the decision to trust you, believe you, hire you, or buy from you happens on your site. It is the backbone, the hub, and the home base of your digital identity.

This chapter explains why your website sits at the center of your brand's ecosystem, how every platform feeds into it, how funnels guide visitors through decision-making, and why the "hub & spoke" model is the foundation of the BrandNameSites system.

WHY ALL ROADS LEAD TO YOUR WEBSITE

People may meet your brand anywhere—Instagram, TikTok, a Google search, a referral, a podcast appearance, or a random recommendation. But their *decision* about you happens in one place: your website.

Your website is where people evaluate:

- Who you are
- What you do
- Why you're qualified
- What you offer
- How you operate
- Whether they can trust you
- Whether you're worth their time or money

Social media sparks curiosity.
Your website closes the deal.

Your Website Is Your Proof of Seriousness

Before someone hires you, they look for proof. They ask themselves:

- "Does this business look organized?"
- "Is this legitimate?"
- "Do they explain things clearly?"
- "Are their services easy to understand?"
- "Do they feel trustworthy?"

Social media can't answer these questions deeply. Posts disappear. Bios are short. Stories vanish. Algorithms bury your content.

But your website is stable, structured, and complete.
It's the only place where your entire brand is represented in full.

Your Website Is the Only Platform You Fully Own

Platforms can change their rules without warning:

- Instagram can hide your posts.
- TikTok can block links.
- Facebook can restrict your reach.
- YouTube can demonetize or delete content.
- Twitter/X can change overnight.
- Entire platforms can disappear—Vine, MySpace, Periscope.

Your website does not suffer these risks. You own:

- The domain
- The hosting
- The content
- The design
- The data
- The experience

It is your single protected digital asset in a constantly shifting environment.

Your Website Is the Home of Your Clarity

Clarity almost never lives on social media.
Social media is too fast, too noisy, too limited.

Clarity lives on the pages where you can:

- Explain your offers
- Address objections
- Show your process
- Display testimonials
- Provide educational content
- Build authority through depth
- Make your brand identity undeniable

Your website is where you tell the *full truth* about your brand.

HOW SOCIAL PLATFORMS FEED YOUR WEBSITE

Most businesses misunderstand social media. They treat platforms like digital storefronts—when in reality, they are digital highways.

Social media is not a destination.
It is a *traffic source*.

Its job is simple:

Create movement → spark curiosity → send people to your website.

Every platform has a traffic pathway:

Instagram → Website

Visual storytelling, brand personality, Reels, and social proof.
People click the link when they want more.

Facebook → Website

Groups, community building, events, and longer explanations.

TikTok → Website

Short, fast, curiosity-driven content that pushes visitors to "learn more."

LinkedIn → Website

Professional authority, credibility, case studies, B2B traffic.

Pinterest → Website

Idea discovery, moodboards, and visual content that directs to blogs and services.

YouTube → Website

Long-form tutorials and evergreen content that nurture deep trust.

Google Business Profile → Website

Local visibility and verification.

In every case, platforms generate interest.
Your website converts interest into action.

THE HUB & SPOKE MODEL

This is the core philosophy that shapes modern digital branding.

Your website is the **hub**.
Everything else is a **spoke**.

The Hub — Your Website:
The center of information, structure, data, and conversion.

Includes:

- Homepage
- Service pages
- About page
- Contact/booking
- Portfolio/work examples

- Blog/resources
- Policies
- Process explanation

The Spokes — Every Other Touchpoint:
Designed solely to drive traffic back to the hub.

Includes:

- Social media posts
- Emails
- Videos
- Paid ads
- Podcasts
- Google results
- Business cards
- Partnerships
- Events
- QR codes

Spokes build attention.
The hub builds conversion.

When the Hub Is Missing

- Audiences get confused
- Messaging becomes scattered
- Trust drops
- Social media feels random
- No matter how hard you post, nothing sticks

When the Hub Is Strong

- Everything feels aligned
- Content becomes easier
- Social media becomes strategic
- Traffic converts faster
- Decisions become clearer
- You stop chasing algorithms

This is why the BrandNameSites system is built around the hub & spoke model. It creates structure, consistency, and control.

FUNNEL STANDARDS: HOW TRAFFIC BECOMES CUSTOMERS

Funnels are not manipulative tactics.
They are guided pathways that help people make confident decisions.

Every brand—large or small—needs at least these three funnel paths.

FUNNEL 1: Awareness → Interest → Website

Step 1: Awareness

Posts, reels, videos, SEO, ads.

Step 2: Interest

Clear messaging that sparks curiosity.

Step 3: Website

Homepage or a targeted landing page.

If this funnel fails, the problem is not the platform—
it's unclear messaging or a weak website.

FUNNEL 2: Value → Proof → Conversion

Step 1: Value

Educational content and tutorials.

Step 2: Proof

Testimonials, case studies, results.

Step 3: Conversion

Booking, checkout, or contact.

This is the funnel that turns visibility into trust.

FUNNEL 3: Warm Traffic → Landing Page → Action

Warm traffic converts fastest because they already know you.

Warm Traffic Sources:

- Email list
- Repeat visitors
- Social followers
- Past clients

Landing Page:

Focused, simple, and fast.

Action:

Book → Buy → Contact → Apply → Download

Warm traffic converts at significantly higher rates when the website is clear.

BRANDNAMESITES FUNNEL RULES

These rules apply to every industry, every brand, every website:

1. **One page = one purpose.**
   Never ask visitors to choose between multiple priorities.
2. **Remove friction.**
   Fewer fields, fewer decisions, fewer distractions.
3. **Consistency converts.**
   If your visual style shifts between platforms and your site, trust collapses.
4. **Make the next step obvious.**
   Confusion kills conversions.
5. **Answer objections upfront.**
   People buy when doubt disappears.
6. **Social media warms the audience.**
   The website converts them.
7. **Funnels evolve over time.**
   As your brand grows, your pathways must adapt.

FINAL THOUGHT FOR THIS CHAPTER

Your website is not a technical requirement.
It is not optional.
It is not an afterthought.

It is the center of your universe—the home of your brand, the container for your clarity, and the engine of your conversions.

Your social platforms are the roads that lead to it.
Your content is the fuel that drives traffic into it.
Your funnels are the structure that turn visitors into customers.

When your digital ecosystem follows the hub & spoke model—and when every piece is connected, intentional, and clear—you gain full control over your presence. You stop depending on algorithms. You stop posting aimlessly. You stop feeling scattered.

You become strategic.
You become consistent.
You become undeniable.

This is why, in the BrandNameSites system…

Your website is—and always will be—the center of the universe.

USER JOURNEY MAPPING

Most business owners believe customers make decisions in a straight line. They imagine someone visits their website, likes what they see, and buys. But in reality, nothing about the digital world is linear. Customers bounce around, compare silently, skim instead of read, and require multiple interactions before they trust anyone enough to take a step.

User journey mapping allows you to finally understand — and guide — how people discover you, evaluate you, return to you, and eventually decide to choose you.

It shows you what people think, feel, want, and fear at each moment of their journey. When you know those moments, you gain control over the entire experience.

No jargon. No complicated diagrams. Just a clear path you can follow.

Every journey moves through a simple flow:

BEGINNING → MIDDLE → END.

But the psychology, the behavior, and the touchpoints in each stage matter more than most brands realize.

Let's break it down.

BEGINNING — "Who are you, and why should I care?"

This is the awareness stage — the moment your brand first appears in someone's world.

What's happening here:

They're seeing you for the first time.
They're comparing you to others.
They're scanning for signs of professionalism.
They're judging your vibe, tone, clarity, and visual coherence.
They're asking, "Is this for me?"

This is not the stage where people buy.
It's where they get curious — or move on.

What they need from you:

- A clear identity
- Quick explanation
- A strong visual impression
- A reason to keep paying attention

This is the moment your brand must interrupt the scroll, earn the pause, and give them enough clarity to continue.

Where this happens:

- Instagram, TikTok, Facebook
- Google search
- Shared content
- Word-of-mouth referrals
- Your homepage
- Your blog
- Your Google Business Profile

Your job in the Beginning phase isn't to sell — it's to earn interest. You must simply show up clearly, consistently, and confidently.

Beginning Stage Psychological Triggers

People respond to three things instantly:

1. Pattern Interrupt

You stop them mid-scroll with a statement that hits.

Examples:

- "Your website is bleeding customers."
- "Stop chasing followers — fix this first."

2. Curiosity

They want to know more.

Examples:

- "The #1 mistake killing your conversions."
- "Why your website loads slowly — and what it's costing you."

3. Relatability

Show that you understand their current struggle.

Examples:

- "Tired of DIY sites that still look DIY?"
- "Feel like your website doesn't match your brand's quality?"

The beginning is about resonance. If it doesn't resonate, the journey stops right here.

MIDDLE — "Do I trust them?"

This is the consideration stage. Now they're comparing, evaluating, analyzing, and deciding if you're even worth remembering.

They're not ready to act yet — but they're gathering evidence.

What's happening here:

They're visiting your website.
They're researching.
They're reading reviews.
They're comparing you to competitors.
They're checking your consistency.
They're silently deciding if you're credible.

This is where most brands lose potential customers — not because the buyer wasn't interested, but because the brand didn't create enough clarity or trust.

What they need from you:

- Simple information
- Clarity, not complexity
- Proof you're reliable
- Testimonials and results
- A professional website structure
- Clean visuals
- Direct, human explanation

Where the Middle phase happens:

- Your website (especially service pages)
- About page
- Case studies
- Testimonials
- Social media content
- YouTube videos
- Blogs
- Email newsletters

Middle Stage Psychological Triggers

These determine whether a visitor moves toward trust or away from you.

4. Social Proof

People trust what other people endorse.

Show testimonials, results, case studies, before/after images, client logos.

5. Authority

People trust experts.

Demonstrate expertise through educational content, certifications, media mentions, or clean, clear explanations.

6. Transparency

People want no hidden surprises.

Show your process, pricing range, timelines, expectations, terms, next steps.

Transparency builds trust faster than hype.

END — "What is the next step?"

This is the decision phase — the moment when interest needs direction.

At this point, they're ready. But readiness still requires clarity.

What's happening here:

They're looking for a place to act.
They're expecting simplicity.
They're checking for any final red flags.
They want reassurance they won't regret choosing you.

What they need from you:

- A clear call-to-action
- Simple forms
- Fast load time
- A sense of safety
- Clear next steps
- A short path to conversion

Where the End phase happens:

- Contact page
- Booking page
- Pricing page
- Checkout
- Application forms
- Your DMs (after the decision is mentally made)

End Stage Psychological Triggers

Three triggers matter most here:

7. Scarcity or Urgency

Only if it's real — fake scarcity breaks trust.

Examples:

- "We only take 5 new clients per month."
- "Spots for Q1 are almost full."

8. Risk Reversal

Show them they won't regret their choice.

Examples:

- Guarantees
- Free revisions
- Clear refund policies
- "If you're not satisfied, we fix it."

9. Clarity

Clarity always wins over cleverness.

- "Book a call."
- "Start your project."
- "Get your audit."
- "Begin now."

Your job is to remove friction so the "yes" feels easy.

THE LADDER OF TOUCHPOINTS

People rarely convert at first contact. In fact, research shows it takes **7–13 touchpoints** before most people are ready to act.

This is the ladder they climb:

1. **Discovery** — They see or hear your name.
2. **Curiosity** — They check your page or profile.
3. **Light Research** — They scroll your content.
4. **Website Visit** — They click your link.
5. **Evaluation** — They read your pages.
6. **Comparison** — They check alternatives.
7. **Decision** — They take action.

The brands that win are the ones who:

- Show up clearly at Step 1
- Build curiosity at Step 2
- Provide value at Step 3
- Convert interest at Step 4
- Remove doubt at Step 5
- Stand out at Step 6
- Make action easy at Step 7

If any step feels confusing, the visitor stops climbing.

HOW PEOPLE ACTUALLY BEHAVE ONLINE

Most businesses design their digital experience based on what they *wish* customers would do — not what they *actually* do.

Here's how people really behave:

1. People skim, they don't read.

Headlines, bullets, spacing, and visuals matter more than paragraphs.

2. People want answers fast.

If they can't find what they want in seconds, they leave.

3. People scroll before clicking.

Your above-the-fold message must be clear.

4. Eyes go top-left first.

Put your value statement where the eyes naturally land.

5. People judge your brand in seconds.

Modern = trustworthy.
Cluttered = confusion.

6. People compare silently.

You won't know when they leave to check competitors.

7. People avoid stress.

Confusing layouts, heavy text, or unclear buttons drive them away.

8. People follow clear paths.

Buttons must be obvious.
Next steps must be simple.

9. People buy when doubt disappears.

The moment they feel certainty, they act.

YOUR JOB: MAP THE JOURNEY AND FILL THE GAPS

User journey mapping is simple:

1. Understand what people need at each stage.
2. Build experiences that give them exactly that.
3. Remove friction and confusion everywhere.

You don't control people — you guide them.

FINAL THOUGHT FOR THIS CHAPTER

User journey mapping isn't complicated. It's human.

It's understanding:

- How people discover brands
- How they evaluate and compare
- What makes them trust
- What makes them hesitate
- What makes them decide
- And what makes them feel confident

When you design your brand around how people *actually* behave, you stop losing customers quietly in the middle of the journey. You stop hoping people will "figure it out." You stop relying on luck.

You guide them.

And that guidance is the difference between brands that struggle...
and brands that convert.

TRUST SYSTEMS & BRAND CREDIBILITY

In the digital world, trust is currency. It determines whether someone chooses your brand, recommends you, or moves on without hesitation. You can have the best design, the best service, the best offering — but without credibility, nothing converts.

People do not buy from brands they do not trust.
And online, trust must be earned quickly, clearly, and consistently.

Strong brands do not wait for trust to "happen."
They design trust intentionally.

This chapter breaks down the trust systems every modern brand must build: social proof, testimonials, case studies, reviews, public relations, authority signals, and your digital footprint. Together, these form the foundation of your credibility — often before anyone ever talks to you directly.

Trust is not optional. Trust is the reason someone chooses you.

WHY TRUST MATTERS MORE THAN EVER

The internet has made expertise easy to fake. Anyone can build a website, create an Instagram account, and claim to be a professional. Customers know this, and they're cautious — often more cautious than brands realize.

Here's the trust gap:

What you know:
You're good at what you do. You deliver value. You mean well.

What the customer knows:
Nothing about you yet.

Your job is to bridge that gap with proof — not with claims, not with hype, but with *evidence*.

Trust is built through signals people can see, verify, and believe.

SOCIAL PROOF: THE FIRST LAYER OF TRUST

Social proof is any public evidence that real people trust you. It is one of the strongest psychological triggers in branding because people believe other people more than they believe marketing messages.

Social proof lowers fear.
It reduces hesitation.
It instantly increases credibility.

Types of Social Proof

Use all that apply:

- Testimonials
- Reviews
- Case studies
- Before/after transformations
- Client logos
- Usage numbers ("100+ clients served")
- Media mentions
- Awards or certifications
- Social engagement
- Word-of-mouth
- Influencer or expert endorsements

Even small forms of social proof matter — screenshots, client messages, or simple before/after improvements.

Why Social Proof Works

It answers the question every customer has:

"Has anyone like me trusted you and gotten real results?"

When people see others having positive experiences, they assume they will too.

Social Proof Standards

Every brand must have social proof placed across:

- Homepage
- Service pages
- About page
- Google Listings
- Landing pages
- Social profiles

If you are not showing social proof, you are forcing your customers to build their own assumptions — and that always leads to doubt.

TESTIMONIALS: HUMANIZED PROOF

Testimonials are short, powerful statements from real clients describing their experience. They are often the first thing people look for on a website or social platform.

What Strong Testimonials Include

A great testimonial answers five questions:

1. *What was the problem?*
2. *Why did they choose you?*
3. *What did you deliver?*
4. *What impressed them?*
5. *What was the result?*

Generic praise means nothing.
Specific outcomes build trust.

Weak Testimonial Example

"They're great to work with!"

Strong Testimonial Example

"BrandNameSites simplified everything. They turned my scattered ideas into a clean, professional website that now brings in steady clients."

Where Testimonials Belong

- Homepage hero section
- Service pages (specific to each service)
- About page
- Contact/booking page
- Sales funnels
- Social posts
- Portfolio/case studies

How to Collect Testimonials

Ask clients at three moments:

- **During the project:** "What has been your favorite part so far?"
- **At completion:** "What would you tell someone considering working with us?"
- **30 days after launch:** "What results have you seen since we launched?"

Make it easy with a simple form or template.

Testimonial Standards

- Aim for at least **5–10 strong testimonials** across your site.
- Use real names, real results, real stories.
- Include photos when possible.
- Keep them updated — old testimonials weaken trust.

CASE STUDIES: DEEP, STRUCTURED EVIDENCE

Case studies are the strongest form of social proof because they reveal transformation, explanation, and real data.

They show someone's journey from struggle → solution → result.

Why Case Studies Matter

People want to see how you work before they ever contact you.

Case studies demonstrate:

- Your thinking
- Your process
- Your ability to solve real problems
- The impact of your work
- Your professionalism
- Your consistency

A Simple Case Study Structure

1. **Client Background**
2. **Problem They Faced**
3. **Your Approach / Solution**
4. **What You Delivered**
5. **Final Results (numbers, insights, outcomes)**
6. **Client Testimonial**

Case Study Example (Condensed)

Client: Local business with outdated website
Problem: Visitors didn't trust their brand
Solution: Rebrand + new website + service clarity
Result: Increase in inquiries, stronger professionalism, higher conversions

Case Study Standards

Every brand should have **2–3 case studies**, even if short.
They add depth behind your claims, showing that you deliver what you promise.

REVIEWS: YOUR PUBLIC SCORE

Reviews are third-party validation — proof you cannot manufacture or manipulate. Customers rely heavily on 리뷰σ for decision-making.

Key Review Platforms

- Google Business Profile
- Yelp
- Facebook
- LinkedIn Recommendations
- Industry-specific directories (G2, Clutch, Houzz, TripAdvisor, etc.)

Why Reviews Matter

They:

- Increase search visibility
- Influence first impressions
- Build instant credibility
- Offer social proof without you lifting a finger
- Affect ranking and reputation
- Provide reassurance before someone contacts you

Review Standards

- Respond within 24–48 hours
- Thank positive reviewers
- Address negative reviews calmly
- Never argue publicly
- Never ignore feedback

How you respond to reviews says as much about your business as the reviews themselves.

Review Benchmarks

To appear credible:

- **10+ reviews minimum**
- **4.5+ star average**
- **Recent reviews within 60–90 days**

Consistency signals activity, engagement, and reliability.

PUBLIC RELATIONS (PR): AUTHORITY & VISIBILITY

PR is not only for large brands. In fact, small businesses often benefit more because visibility helps them stand out in crowded markets.

PR builds trust through association and credibility.

Forms of PR

- Interviews
- Podcast guesting
- Local features
- Magazine articles
- Press releases
- Awards
- Speaking engagements
- Community involvement

Why PR Works

It provides:

- Authority
- Legitimacy
- Visibility
- Professionalism
- External validation

People trust what the media trusts.

PR Standards

Aim for:

- **1–2 features per year**
- **1 consistent platform you show up on**
- **1 form of community involvement**

PR compounds over time — the more you show up, the more credible you become.

CREDIBILITY THROUGH EXPERTISE

Trust is not only built through social proof — it's built through demonstrated expertise.

Ways to Show Expertise

- Publish original research
- Share detailed how-to content
- Teach, not tease
- Offer real insights
- Speak at events
- Host webinars
- Appear on podcasts
- Write blog posts with depth
- Create guides and educational resources
- Share behind-the-scenes process
- Be transparent about limitations

Thought leadership is credibility in action.

THE DIGITAL FOOTPRINT SCORECARD

Your brand's public reputation — measured.

Your digital footprint includes every trace of your brand online. Strong brands actively monitor and maintain this footprint. Weak brands ignore it — and lose trust without realizing it.

Here is the BrandNameSites Digital Footprint Scorecard:

1. Google Search Presence

- Does your business appear?
- Is your information accurate?
- Are reviews visible and positive?
- Are recent photos showing?
- Do positive links outweigh negative ones?

2. Social Media Audit

- Are profiles consistent across platforms?
- Are visuals professional?
- Is messaging aligned?
- Is there recent activity?
- Do posts reflect value and clarity?

3. Website Quality

- Is your site fast, modern, and mobile-friendly?
- Does it follow your brand identity?
- Does it showcase trust signals?
- Is your message clear?

4. Public Listings

- Google, Yelp, Bing, industry directories
- Accurate contact info?
- Hours correct?
- Duplicate or outdated listings removed?

5. Content Presence

- Educational content available?
- Case studies or testimonials visible?
- Blog or resource center active?
- Helpful posts across platforms?

6. Customer Feedback Systems

- Testimonials collected regularly
- Case studies published
- Recent reviews visible
- Clear feedback loops

7. Professional Footprint

- Press mentions?
- Speaking engagements?
- Community involvement?
- Positive mentions from others?

8. Brand Consistency

- Visuals aligned across platforms
- Tone unified across all channels
- Messaging identical everywhere

THE TRUST STACK: LAYERING PROOF

Strong brands layer trust signals so credibility hits from multiple angles.

A full trust stack includes:

- Testimonials
- Case studies
- Reviews
- Client logos
- Credentials
- Awards
- Expert commentary
- Numbers and statistics
- PR features
- Community involvement
- Social engagement
- Before/after examples

Each layer strengthens the others.

FINAL THOUGHT FOR THIS CHAPTER

Credibility is not built by accident.
It is built through systems — consistently, intentionally, and publicly.

Trust is the foundation of a strong brand.
Credibility is the structure that holds it up.

When your brand uses:

- Social proof
- Testimonials
- Case studies
- Reviews
- PR

- Authority content
- A clean digital footprint

…you become the obvious choice. Not because you said so — but because the evidence says so for you.

Trust built intentionally becomes trust built permanently.

PART V – BUILDING & MAINTAINING A DIGITAL BRAND

THE BRAND MAINTENANCE PLAN

A strong brand is not a one-time achievement — it is a living system.

Most businesses launch a brand, build a website, post some content, and then drift into silence. Weeks turn into months. Social pages go stale. Website information becomes outdated. What was once polished slowly feels abandoned.

A neglected brand is a brand losing trust.

Maintenance is not optional.
Maintenance is the difference between brands that stay relevant and brands that silently fall behind.

This chapter gives you the **BrandNameSites Maintenance Plan** — an ongoing routine that keeps your website, visuals, content, and digital presence sharp, modern, and trustworthy all year long.

Think of it like maintaining a home or a car:
If you don't check it, it breaks.
If you maintain it, it lasts.

A brand that is maintained is a brand that stays chosen.

THE MAINTENANCE MINDSET

Your brand is a living system. It grows, shifts, ages, and sometimes drifts without you noticing. Digital assets naturally degrade over time:

Technical degradation

- Plugins need updates
- Security vulnerabilities appear
- Links break
- Images fail to load
- Forms stop submitting
- Uptime drops
- Page speed slows as content grows

Content degradation

- Information becomes outdated
- Services evolve
- Pricing changes
- Testimonials get old
- Blog posts become irrelevant
- Competitors publish fresher content

Perception degradation

- Design trends shift
- Customer expectations change
- Your brand tone evolves
- Your visuals feel inconsistent
- A 2022 website no longer looks like a 2025 brand

If you do not maintain your brand, you fall behind even if you don't realize it's happening.

Maintenance is not glamorous…
but it's the reason strong brands stay strong.

THE BRANDNAMESITES QUARTERLY MAINTENANCE CHECKLIST

Every 3 months, your brand should undergo a structured review.
Quarterly maintenance keeps you ahead instead of behind.

1. Website Review

Review every major page with a fresh set of eyes:

- Is any information outdated?
- Are your services still accurate?
- Do prices reflect your current offer?
- Have any links broken?
- Do all buttons and forms work?
- Does your mobile layout look clean on multiple devices?
- Does your homepage still communicate clearly?
- Are load times under 3 seconds?

If something feels outdated, unclear, or unused — fix or remove it.

2. Visual Consistency Review

Check whether your brand still looks aligned:

- Are your primary colors used consistently?
- Are fonts uniform across platforms?
- Are templates being followed?
- Do new graphics match your brand kit?
- Any visuals look outdated or off-brand?

Remove old graphics that no longer reflect your identity.

3. Content Audit

Look at your recent content:

- What performed well?
- What fell flat?
- What feels outdated?
- What can be repurposed?
- What topics are missing?
- Are you still using your signature language consistently?

A quarterly content audit prevents clutter and brings clarity.

4. SEO & Search Visibility

- Google your business
- Ensure your information is correct
- Update Google Business Profile
- Read and respond to new reviews
- Check if pages are indexed
- Verify your sitemap is clean
- Watch for any ranking drops

If search results look messy, confusing, or outdated — fix them immediately.

5. Social Media Alignment

- Update bios and profile photos
- Ensure links are current
- Pin updated highlights or posts
- Remove outdated posts if necessary
- Confirm graphics match your brand identity

Your social media should look like an extension of your website — not a separate universe.

6. System Health

Every quarter:

- Update plugins
- Update themes
- Confirm SSL certificate is valid
- Review hosting performance
- Update integrations (email, CRM, analytics)
- Remove unused tools that may cause conflict

A healthy system leads to a healthy brand.

Quarterly Goal

Keep your brand clean, current, and consistent.

VISUAL REFRESH STANDARDS

A visual refresh is not a rebrand — it is maintenance.

Your brand should evolve intentionally without losing identity.
Think of it as upgrading the edges while keeping the core.

When to Refresh Your Visuals

Refresh when:

- Your audience shifts
- Your services evolve
- Your design begins to feel outdated
- Your content looks inconsistent
- Your spacing or typography needs refining

Most brands need a visual refresh every **12–18 months** — not a full rebrand.

What a Visual Refresh Includes

- Updated spacing rules
- Cleaner layout templates
- Better photography style
- Improved hierarchy
- Modernized icons
- Refined color usage
- Updated secondary palette
- Stronger typography pairings

What a Visual Refresh Does NOT Mean

- New logo
- New colors
- New identity system
- Starting from scratch

You are not changing who you are.
You are elevating how you show up.

WEBSITE UPDATE CADENCE

Your website is not a brochure — it is a living, evolving part of your business. It should never sit untouched.

Below is the BrandNameSites cadence for keeping your site current.

Monthly Tasks

- Update your blog or resource center
- Publish new content
- Check for broken links
- Remove outdated announcements
- Test all forms
- Do a quick mobile check
- Add new testimonial screenshots or reviews
- Update portfolio or recent work

Quarterly Tasks

- Re-read every service page
- Update features, benefits, pricing
- Refresh imagery or hero sections
- Adjust spacing for modern feel
- Add case studies
- Test checkout or booking flows
- Clean up old files and media
- Improve your About page with fresh language

Bi-Annual Tasks (Every 6 Months)

- Review homepage messaging
- Run a speed test and fix slow areas
- Update any outdated photography
- Improve page structure for clarity
- Reevaluate your brand story
- Add new trust signals
- Update the footer and navigation if needed

Annual Tasks

- Conduct a full website audit
- Evaluate design against modern standards
- Review every page for alignment
- Conduct a full accessibility check
- Update your entire resource library
- Review hosting performance and security
- Refresh homepage visuals and copy

Standard

Your website should **never go 6 months without a review** and **never go 12 months without improvement.**

ANALYTICS TRACKING FOR BRAND HEALTH

You don't need to be a data analyst to understand your brand — you only need to track the right numbers.

Below are the **BrandNameSites Analytics Standards.**

1. Website Analytics — Monthly

Track:

- Page views
- Bounce rate
- Average time on page
- Top performing pages
- Top exit pages
- Mobile vs. desktop traffic
- Form submissions
- Button clicks
- Conversion goals

What These Numbers Reveal

- What people care about
- What people ignore
- Where they get confused
- Where they drop off
- What brings them back
- What needs improvement

2. Social Media Analytics — Monthly

Track:

- Engagement rate
- Saves (most important)
- Shares
- Link clicks
- Profile visits
- Reach vs. followers

What These Numbers Reveal

Visibility ≠ interest.
Engagement ≠ trust.
Followers ≠ conversions.

Trust comes from clarity, consistency, and credibility — not vanity metrics.

3. Content Analytics — Quarterly

Track:

- Top saved posts
- Most shared content
- Topics generating the highest interest
- Formats that perform best
- Which content drives website clicks

What These Numbers Reveal

Likes are shallow.
Comments are nice.
Shares and saves show belief.

Those signals show what your audience cares about deeply.

4. Funnel Analytics — Quarterly

Track:

- Where users drop off
- High-intent pages
- Low-intent behavior
- What pages convert best
- What CTAs get clicked
- Which audiences take action

What These Numbers Reveal

Your funnel will always tell the truth:

Your website either guides people…
or loses them.

WEEKLY, MONTHLY, QUARTERLY, & ANNUAL MAINTENANCE — FULL PLAN

This is the complete BrandNameSites Maintenance Schedule.

WEEKLY (15–30 minutes)

- Check and respond to contact forms
- Respond to reviews within 24–48 hours
- Post or schedule content on social media
- Monitor website uptime
- Check for major errors
- Respond to all DMs and comments
- Check site speed briefly

MONTHLY (1–2 hours)

- Update website content
- Perform analytics review
- Publish 1–2 blog posts
- Check broken links
- Backup website
- Update software, plugins, and themes
- Add new testimonials or case studies
- Optimize one piece of content

QUARTERLY (2–4 hours)

- Full analytics deep dive
- SEO audit
- Competitor review
- Email list cleanup
- Social media audit
- Update Google Business Profile
- Review service pages
- Add new portfolio pieces
- Fix outdated statements
- Improve one major page

ANNUALLY (Full Day)

- Website refresh evaluation
- Brand consistency audit
- Content inventory and pruning
- Digital footprint review
- Security and performance overhaul
- Rewrite core copy if needed
- Update team photos and bios
- Modernize homepage
- Review brand kit rules

Annual reviews keep your brand alive, relevant, and competitive.

WHEN TO REFRESH VS. REDESIGN YOUR WEBSITE

Minor Refresh — Every 12–18 Months

Update:

- Typography
- Spacing
- Hero section
- Color accents
- Imagery
- Testimonials
- Messaging
- Buttons and CTAs

Major Redesign — Every 3–5 Years

Do this when:

- The design looks outdated
- Technology is old
- Speed is slow
- Brand has pivoted
- Competitors look significantly better
- Conversion rates have dropped

A redesign is not dramatic.
It is necessary.

FINAL THOUGHT FOR THIS CHAPTER

A brand doesn't stay strong because it was built perfectly.
It stays strong because it is maintained deliberately.

Your maintenance plan is your insurance policy.
Your routine is your reputation.
Your consistency is your professionalism.

When you follow this plan, your brand stays sharp, modern, credible, and trustworthy — year after year.

A strong maintenance plan protects your brand today
and prepares it for growth tomorrow.

SCALING YOUR PRESENCE

Scaling your presence doesn't mean posting more, doing more, or exhausting yourself trying to "keep up." It means growing intentionally — with clarity, structure, and systems that allow your brand to expand without losing its identity.

Growth done right is strategic.
Growth done poorly becomes chaos.

Scaling is not about becoming bigger.
It's about becoming **stronger, smarter, and more efficient**, without lowering the standards you worked so hard to build.

This chapter breaks down the five pillars of scaling your presence:

- When to rebrand
- When to expand
- How to manage multi-brand ecosystems
- What to automate
- How to build a team that protects your brand

Scaling is not something that happens to you — it is something you decide.

WHEN TO REBRAND

Rebranding is not a mood swing or a reaction to boredom. It is a strategic decision made only when your current brand no longer represents who you are or where you're going.

A rebrand should happen because you've outgrown your identity — not because you feel like changing your colors or chasing a trend.

You Should Rebrand When:

1. Your audience has changed.

The people you serve today are not the people you served when you started.

2. Your offer has evolved.

You've entered a different market or elevated your services.

3. Your visuals look outdated.

If your brand looks older than your industry demands, trust will slip.

4. Your identity no longer aligns with your goals.

You've matured — but your brand is still stuck in its "early days."

5. Confusion is happening.

If your brand no longer communicates clearly, you're losing opportunities.

These are strategic reasons — grounded in growth.

When NOT to Rebrand

- Because you're bored
- Because trends shifted
- Because a competitor rebranded
- Because you're hoping it will fix a struggling business
- Because you want "something fresh"

A rebrand is not therapy.
A rebrand is strategy.

The Rebrand Decision Framework

Ask yourself:

1. Has our business fundamentally changed?
2. Has our audience significantly shifted?
3. Does our current brand cause confusion?
4. Is our brand actively hurting growth?
5. Does our branding look outdated compared to competitors?

If you answered yes to 3 or more: It's time.

If you answered yes to 1 or 2: Consider a visual refresh, not a full rebuild.

If you answered no to all: Grow your presence — not your identity.

Standard

Rebranding should be done every **5–10 years**, only when your company has outgrown itself — not because you're tired of your logo.

WHEN TO EXPAND

Expansion is not about adding complexity.
It is about adding value.

You expand when your brand foundation is strong enough to support growth — not when you're trying to patch holes.

You Should Expand When:

1. Demand is higher than your capacity.

You're turning down work or working beyond healthy limits.

2. Your processes are predictable and repeatable.

If your delivery model still depends entirely on you guessing, you are not ready.

3. Your audience wants more from you.

There is proven demand — not imagined demand.

4. You have a strategic reason to grow.

Your expansion aligns with the direction of your business.

5. Your brand identity is stable and consistent.

Expansion multiplies whatever already exists — clarity or confusion.

Forms of Expansion

- New services
- Digital products or downloads
- Workshops, events, or courses
- New markets or locations
- New customer segments
- Licensing or partnerships

Standard

Expand only when your current brand is **working**, not when you're trying to "fix" something.

Expansion should amplify strength, not noise.

MULTI-BRAND STRATEGY

Some businesses eventually reach a point where one brand cannot contain everything. This is where multi-brand strategy becomes beneficial — or destructive, depending on how it's handled.

Multi-brand ecosystems require discipline, clarity, and structure.

When Multi-Brand Strategy Makes Sense

1. You serve more than one distinct audience.

Different audiences require different tones, visuals, or language.

2. You offer services that cannot fit under one identity.

Some offers need autonomy.

3. You need separation to avoid confusing customers.

One size does not fit all.

4. A parent brand cannot carry every direction.

Some things need their own house.

Common Multi-Brand Mistakes

- Creating too many brands too fast
- Running multiple brands with no shared structure
- Inconsistent visuals across brands
- Diluting your primary brand
- Creating brands based on excitement instead of strategy

The BrandNameSites Rule

One parent brand. Multiple child brands. One unified strategy.

This means:

- One primary identity (your company)
- Child brands underneath with their own visuals
- Centralized systems and standards
- Shared processes
- Clear differentiation with clear connection

Multi-brand strategy is not a playground — it is architecture.
Build it carefully.

AUTOMATIONS THAT MATTER

You cannot scale manually.
You cannot grow by adding more work to the same hours.

Automation is not about removing the human touch — it is about removing repetitive tasks so you can focus on strategy, creativity, and quality.

Automation protects your energy and preserves consistency.

Automations Every Brand Should Implement

1. Email Sequences

Automate:

- Welcome sequences
- Onboarding
- Lead nurturing
- Follow-up reminders
- Post-purchase guidance

2. Appointment Scheduling

Stop the back-and-forth.
Automated booking saves hours every month.

3. CRM Systems

Track:

- Leads
- Clients
- Tasks
- Follow-ups
- Conversations

A CRM prevents lost opportunities.

4. Social Media Systems

Systems, not mindless posting:

- Monthly content planning
- Template-based creation
- Automated scheduling
- Content libraries

5. Website Automations

- Contact form routing
- Lead tagging
- Automated downloads
- Inquiry confirmation
- Follow-up emails
- Cart recovery sequences

6. Payment Automations

- Invoicing
- Subscription billing
- Receipts
- Late reminders
- Automated bookkeeping integrations

Automation does not replace relationship — it supports it.

Standard

Automate tasks.
Do not automate your humanity.

TEAM BUILDING: SCALING WITH PEOPLE

At some point, you will reach your capacity.
Your brand outgrows your ability to do everything alone.

That's when team building becomes part of scaling — not before.

You Should Hire When:

- You're consistently overwhelmed
- Quality is slipping
- You're losing opportunities
- You need specialized skills
- Growth is happening faster than you can sustain

Hiring too early causes chaos.
Hiring too late causes burnout.

Who to Hire First

1. Assistant / Coordinator

Handles:

- Admin
- Email
- Scheduling
- Follow-up
- Organization

They protect your time.

2. Social Media / Content Support

They execute your content — **not your strategy** — using your templates and standards.

3. Designer or Developer

Helps with:

- Updates
- Upgrades
- Campaigns
- Website improvements

4. Project Manager (Later Stage)

When you need someone to manage:

- Workflows
- Team roles
- Client communication
- Deadlines
- Quality control

Standards for Team Building

Every team member must:

- Follow brand guidelines
- Understand your identity
- Use your templates
- Respect your tone and voice
- Contribute to clarity
- Protect your standards

A team amplifies your strengths — and your weaknesses.
Do not scale your team before you scale your clarity.

GROWING WITHOUT LOSING YOUR BRAND

As brands scale, the biggest risk is **dilution**.

How brands get diluted:

- Chasing every opportunity
- Offering too many services
- Inconsistent quality
- Hiring people who don't understand the brand
- Trying to be everything to everyone

How to protect your brand during growth:

- Stay focused on your core
- Document your processes
- Hire people who get your values
- Follow your brand guidelines
- Say no often
- Maintain quality control

A strong brand is not loud — it is consistent.

FINAL THOUGHT FOR THIS CHAPTER

Scaling is not about becoming bigger — it's about becoming clearer, smarter, and more intentional.

Rebranding brings clarity.
Expansion brings opportunity.
Multi-brand strategy brings structure.
Automation brings efficiency.
Team building brings sustainability.

Scaling is a strategic movement — not an emotional reaction.

When you scale with intention, your brand becomes more stable, more recognizable, and more prepared for long-term success.

You don't scale by doing more.
You scale by doing what matters.

MISTAKES BRANDS MUST AVOID

A strong brand isn't built only by what you do right—
but by what you refuse to do wrong.

Brand failure rarely happens in one dramatic moment.
It happens quietly, slowly, invisibly… through small mistakes that weaken identity, confuse customers, and damage credibility long before the business realizes what went wrong.

This chapter is your warning system.
These are the mistakes that separate strong, stable brands from struggling, inconsistent ones.
Avoid them, and your brand will grow with clarity.
Ignore them, and your brand will collapse under confusion.

Below is the **improved, expanded, unified BrandNameSites list of critical branding mistakes**, drawn from real businesses, real patterns, and real failures.

SECTION 1 — FOUNDATION & IDENTITY MISTAKES

What you build at the beginning determines what you become later.

These mistakes sit at the root of every branding struggle.
If the foundation is weak, nothing else can stand.

1. Starting with a logo instead of strategy

The classic mistake.
People rush to design a logo before defining:

- Their purpose
- Their values
- Their audience
- Their positioning
- The problem they solve

A logo is an expression of a brand—not the creation of one.

2. Having no clear target audience

If you say,
"My service is for everyone,"
you've already lost.

Brands that try to serve everyone end up serving no one.

3. No clear positioning or differentiation

If your brand sounds like every competitor, customers default to:

- Whoever is cheaper
- Whoever answers faster
- Whoever feels more trustworthy

Positioning is how you become the "obvious choice."

4. Copying competitors

Businesses think,
"Well, they're successful—so I'll do that too."

But copies never win.
You become forgettable, unoriginal, and invisible.

5. Constantly changing your brand direction

Frequent changes signal instability and confuse your audience.
A stable identity builds trust.

6. Using trends instead of strategy

Trendy branding looks great for six months and embarrassing a year later.
Strategy lasts.

7. Weak brand story or none at all

Customers connect to human stories—not technical descriptions.

8. No signature language or recognizable voice

Your brand should *sound* like you in every message.
If your tone shifts everywhere, people won't trust it.

9. Values that don't match actions

Brands lose credibility when they claim one thing and behave another way.
Customers always notice.

10. Building your business on rented land

Brands built entirely on Instagram, TikTok, or Facebook live at the mercy of algorithms.
Without a website, you're building someone else's platform—not your own.

SECTION 2 — WEBSITE & DIGITAL PRESENCE MISTAKES

Your website is your home base. If it's broken, outdated, or unclear, your brand is broken too.

These are the mistakes that silently kill conversions.

11. Outdated or low-quality website

Looks old = feels untrustworthy.

12. Slow loading speed

53% of users abandon a site that loads in over 3 seconds.
Speed is a trust signal.

13. Not mobile-friendly

Most visitors are on mobile.
If your site breaks on phones, your brand breaks too.

14. Cluttered or confusing homepage

A homepage should answer:

- What you do
- Who you serve
- Why it matters
- What to do next

in seconds.

15. No clear call-to-action

If you don't guide people, they won't move.

16. Poor spacing, layout, or visual hierarchy

Spacing *is* part of your brand.
Clutter = cheap.
Clean = confident.

17. Too much text or unclear messaging

People skim, not read.
Your copy must be:

- Short
- Clear
- Structured
- Intentional

18. Broken links or outdated pages

Nothing destroys trust faster than clicking something that leads nowhere.

19. No testimonials or social proof

People don't believe brands—they believe other customers.

20. Inactive or outdated social profiles

If your last post was six months ago, people assume you're unprofessional or out of business.

21. No SSL certificate ("Not Secure" warning)

Customers won't trust a site their browser tells them to avoid.

22. Generic stock photos

Stock photos feel fake.
Original imagery builds trust.

23. No contact information or hidden details

If customers struggle to reach you, they won't trust you.

24. Outdated copyright year

A tiny detail with a huge implication.
If your site says "© 2021," customers assume you're not maintaining anything.

SECTION 3 — CONTENT & SOCIAL MEDIA MISTAKES

Content is the voice of your brand. If it's inconsistent, unclear, or random, your brand feels the same.

25. Posting without a strategy

Random content = random results.

26. Content that doesn't match your identity

Your visuals, tone, and topics must reinforce your brand—not contradict it.

27. Overusing trends that don't fit your brand

Trends attract attention but rarely build trust.
Use sparingly.

28. Writing captions that are too long, too vague, or complicated

People scroll fast.
Your content must hook and help.

29. Using inconsistent templates or colors

Visual instability makes your brand forgettable.

30. Sounding robotic or generic

Your brand voice should feel human—never corporate or stiff.

31. Not providing value

Selling without educating makes people tune out.

32. Ignoring questions your customer asks

If people ask you the same things repeatedly, answer them visibly in your content.

33. Posting only sales messages

Nobody follows a constant advertisement.

34. Cross-posting the exact same content everywhere

Each platform has its own culture.
Copy-paste content underperforms.

35. Neglected social profiles

Unanswered comments, ignored messages, no engagement—
these destroy trust more than you realize.

36. No content variety

Your audience needs education, inspiration, clarity, and proof—not one flavor forever.

SECTION 4 — TRUST & CREDIBILITY MISTAKES

Trust is the foundation of every purchase. Lose it, and nothing else matters.

37. No testimonials

People don't trust businesses that offer no proof.

38. Generic testimonials

"Great service!" means nothing.
Specifics build credibility.

39. No reviews

If a business has zero reviews in 2025, it's a red flag.

40. Ignoring negative reviews

Silence looks like guilt.
Respond professionally and promptly.

41. No case studies or transformation stories

Case studies show process, results, and real outcomes.
They close the gap between interest and decision.

42. No clear pricing (or hiding costs)

Customers distrust brands that avoid transparency.

43. Using an unprofessional email address

A business using Gmail looks small and unreliable.

44. Making promises you can't keep

Overpromising leads to refunds, bad reviews, and broken trust.

SECTION 5 — CUSTOMER EXPERIENCE & PROCESS MISTAKES

Most brands don't lose customers because of quality—they lose them because of experience.

45. Slow response times

A 3-day response time is a fast way to lose customers.

46. Complicated onboarding

Confusing steps create friction and regret.

47. Inconsistent communication style

Your voice should feel the same across email, text, website, and social.

48. Overpromising and underdelivering

Breaking expectations destroys trust faster than anything else.

49. No clear client process

If clients don't know what's coming next, they feel anxious and unprepared.

50. Poor follow-up or no follow-up

Follow-up is part of customer experience—not an optional step.

51. Forgetting past customers

A lack of post-project support costs you:

- referrals
- repeat business
- long-term loyalty

52. No automation to support efficiency

Manual systems collapse as you grow.

SECTION 6 — PRICING, POSITIONING & GROWTH MISTAKES

Growth magnifies both strengths and weaknesses. If your foundation is unstable, growth will break it.

53. Competing on price instead of value

Competing on price is a race to the bottom.

54. No transparent pricing structure

Customers hate mystery pricing.

55. Discounting too quickly

You condition customers to negotiate everything.

56. Trying to serve everyone

Generalists struggle.
Specialists thrive.

57. Growing too fast

Rapid expansion without structure causes:

- poor delivery
- unhappy clients
- ruined reputation

58. Not delegating when overwhelmed

"You do everything" is not a business plan.

59. No documented processes

Without systems, scaling becomes chaos.

60. Not reinvesting back into the business

Brands die when they stop evolving.

SECTION 7 — WARNING SIGNS YOUR BRAND IS LOSING ALIGNMENT

These red flags tell you something deeper is wrong.

Identity Warning Signs

- You feel tempted to redesign constantly
- People misunderstand what you do
- Your visuals don't match across platforms
- Your tone changes everywhere

Website Warning Signs

- Visitors leave quickly
- Your site embarrasses you
- You get fewer inquiries
- People ask simple questions your site should answer

Content Warning Signs

- You never know what to post
- No saves, shares, or meaningful engagement
- Your voice sounds different every week
- You're posting out of panic, not purpose

Customer Experience Warning Signs

- Clients feel confused
- You spend too much time explaining things
- You lose leads after first contact
- You keep getting the same complaints

Business Warning Signs

- You're overwhelmed and stretched thin
- New ideas distract you from finishing the old ones
- Systems break every time more customers arrive
- You're expanding without clarity

If you see **three or more** of these signs, your brand has drifted from its standards.

SECTION 8 — THE COST OF IGNORING STANDARDS

Ignoring branding standards is never harmless.
It always costs something—and usually more than you think.

1. Loss of Trust

Inconsistency creates doubt.
Doubt kills conversions.

2. Lower Conversion Rates

Confusion = hesitation
Hesitation = no sale

3. Wasted Money

Brands without clarity:

- redesign constantly
- rewrite endlessly
- rebuild repeatedly

You spend more trying to fix what standards would prevent.

4. Weak Online Presence

Inconsistency destroys memorability.

5. Customer Drop-Off

When paths are unclear or websites outdated, people disappear silently.

6. Poor Data and Decisions

Without clarity, analytics can't guide improvement.

7. Scaling Becomes Impossible

Weak identity + weak systems = growth collapse.

8. Reputation Damage

One off-brand message can undo months of hard work.

SECTION 9 — REAL-WORLD EXAMPLES (BASED ON COMMON PATTERNS)

Example 1: The "Pretty but Broken" Brand

Beautiful visuals. Stunning logo.
But the website? Slow. Confusing. Disorganized.

Result:
People compliment the aesthetics—
but never buy.

Example 2: The Trend Chaser

Changes branding every six months based on Instagram trends.

Result:
Zero recognition.
Zero stability.
Zero brand equity.

Example 3: The Invisible Expert

Extremely talented.
Never posts valuable content.

Result:
Competitors with half their skill take the spotlight.

Example 4: The Crowded Website

Every badge, every award, every paragraph crammed on the homepage.

Result:
Visitors get overwhelmed and leave.

Example 5: The Multi-Brand Multitasker

Three brands launched at once.
None with clear structure.

Result:
Confusion. Overwhelm.
No growth anywhere.

FINAL THOUGHT FOR THIS CHAPTER

Brands don't collapse overnight.
They crumble through small, silent mistakes:

- inconsistency
- confusion
- neglect
- emotional decisions
- ignored standards

Your brand becomes strong when your choices stay aligned.
You protect your brand by avoiding the mistakes that pull it apart.

A strong brand is not perfect—
but it is **consistent**, clear, stable, and intentional.

Avoid the mistakes.
Honor your standards.
And your brand will stand out in a way that lasts.

PART VI – BLUEPRINTS, TEMPLATES & AUDITS

THE BRAND AUDIT FRAMEWORK

You cannot fix what you do not measure — and you cannot grow what you do not evaluate.

A brand audit is one of the most powerful tools you can use to evaluate your identity, presence, and performance. It shows you what's working, what's breaking, and what needs refinement. Without an audit, brands operate on emotion instead of strategy, assuming everything looks fine simply because nothing is on fire.

Brands don't fall apart in dramatic moments — they drift silently.
An audit prevents the drift.

This chapter introduces the **BrandNameSites 360° Audit System**, a complete framework to measure brand strength through identity, visuals, website performance, digital presence, user experience, content, trust, consistency, and long-term health.

This system combines:

1. **The 50-Point Brand Audit** — overall brand health
2. **The Website Audit Checklist** — technical, UX, and conversion quality
3. **The Digital Presence Scorecard** — your visibility, activity, and relevance
4. **The Brand Consistency Meter** — alignment across every touchpoint
5. **An Action Plan Blueprint** — turning audit results into real progress

A brand that audits itself stays sharp.
A brand that ignores audits becomes inconsistent without noticing.

This chapter gives you the complete system.

SECTION 1 — HOW TO USE THE AUDIT FRAMEWORK

Before you begin, understand the purpose:

An audit is not about perfection.
It's about clarity.

Step 1: Complete the audit honestly

Don't grade anything based on plans, intentions, or wishes. Audit what exists today.

Step 2: Calculate your score

This gives you a snapshot of brand health.

Step 3: Identify your weakest areas

These are the gaps that cost you consistency, credibility, and conversion.

Step 4: Prioritize fixes

Start with high-impact issues:

- clarity issues
- trust issues
- website issues
- inconsistency issues

Step 5: Reaudit in 90 days

Brands evolve. Audits must evolve with them.

SECTION 2 — THE BRANDNAMESITES 50-POINT BRAND AUDIT

This is the official 50-point audit used to evaluate the full scope of a brand.

Mark each item as:

✓ Yes
✗ No
⚠ Needs Attention

Or rate from 0–2 if you prefer numerical scoring:

0 = Not implemented
1 = Needs work
2 = Fully implemented

IDENTITY & POSITIONING (1–10)

Your brand identity sets the foundation for everything else.
A strong identity is clear, confident, and recognizable.

1. Your brand purpose is clear
2. Your vision is defined and inspiring
3. Your values are documented and practiced
4. Your audience is clearly identified
5. Your positioning differentiates you
6. Your signature language is consistent
7. Your brand voice is recognizable
8. Your tone matches your audience
9. Your story is clear and easy to tell
10. Your message is consistent everywhere

VISUAL IDENTITY (11–20)

Visual instability is one of the top reasons brands look unprofessional.

11. Logo is used consistently
12. Color palette is documented
13. Typography system is consistent
14. Spacing guidelines are followed
15. Imagery style is recognizable
16. Templates match brand identity
17. Icons/illustrations follow one style
18. Brand kit is used everywhere
19. No outdated visuals remain in circulation
20. **Visual identity feels modern and aligned**

CONTENT QUALITY (21–30)

Content is the voice of your identity. It must feel intentional — not random.

21. Content aligns with your brand voice
22. Content provides value, not noise
23. Educational content exists
24. Story-based content exists
25. Promotional content is balanced
26. Content supports your niche
27. Content avoids contradictions
28. Captions are clear and on-brand
29. Content has structure and predictability
30. **Your content demonstrates expertise**

CUSTOMER EXPERIENCE (31–40)

Poor experience breaks trust faster than poor design.

31. Inquiries receive fast responses
32. Onboarding is documented and simple
33. Communication is consistent
34. Your process is easy to follow
35. Clients rarely report confusion
36. Offboarding is smooth and professional
37. Testimonials collected regularly
38. Case studies updated regularly
39. Reviews monitored and responded to
40. **Customer experience matches your values**

WEBSITE PRESENCE (41–45)

Your website is your digital headquarters. If it fails, your brand fails.

41. Messaging is clear and simple
42. Navigation is predictable
43. Mobile-first design works across devices
44. Pages load quickly
45. Calls-to-action are consistent

DIGITAL ECOSYSTEM (46–50)

Your digital presence must feel unified.

46. Google Business Profile is accurate
47. Social media profiles are aligned
48. All platform links work
49. Your digital footprint is positive
50. **Brand identity matches everywhere**

SECTION 3 — WEBSITE AUDIT CHECKLIST

A website audit is not about aesthetics. It's about clarity, credibility, speed, and conversion.

This is the BrandNameSites Standard.

1. Homepage

- Clear above-the-fold message
- Simple headline + subheadline
- Strong, visible CTA
- Clean layout and spacing
- Mobile view optimized
- No clutter or distractions

2. Navigation

- Predictable menu structure
- Limited categories
- Dropdowns used sparingly
- Clear footer organization

3. Service Pages

- Clear explanations
- Simple "what's included" section
- Transparent pricing or starting prices
- Testimonials present
- CTA at top and bottom

4. About Page

- Clear brand story
- Professional photo or visual
- Clear values
- Why you exist + who you serve

5. Contact Page

- Simple form
- Clear next steps
- Mobile-friendly
- Email and alternate contact options
- Confirmation or auto-response

6. Technical & Performance

- SSL certificate active
- Load time under 3 seconds
- Compressed images/media
- No broken links
- Updated plugins/integrations

7. User Experience

- Consistent button styles
- Clear sections
- Strong visual hierarchy
- Easy-to-read typography
- Sufficient white space

8. Content Quality

- Up-to-date information
- No outdated announcements
- Simple language
- No unnecessary jargon

9. Accessibility

- Alt text on images
- High color contrast
- Readable font sizes
- Labels on all forms

10. Conversion

- CTA repeated across pages
- Simple next steps
- No information overload
- Logical funnel flow

SECTION 4 — DIGITAL PRESENCE SCORECARD

Rate each from 1–5:
1 = Needs Improvement
5 = Excellent / Aligned

1. Identity Score
Clarity and consistency across all platforms.

2. Visual Score
Modern, aligned, and recognizable.

3. Website Score
Professional, fast, clear, and converting.

4. Content Score
Consistent, educational, branded.

5. Engagement Score
Responsiveness, tone, consistency.

6. Trust Score
Reviews, testimonials, case studies.

7. Presence Score
Visibility, activity, credibility across the web.

8. User Experience Score
Navigation, clarity, support, journey.

Total Score (40 possible)

- **35–40:** Exceptional
- **28–34:** Strong but needs refinement
- **20–27:** Misaligned
- **Below 20:** High risk, low clarity

SECTION 5 — BRAND CONSISTENCY METER

Consistency builds trust faster than anything else.

Rate each:

✓ Always
~ Sometimes
✗ Never

Identity Consistency

- Our purpose and message are clear
- Tone sounds the same everywhere
- Our brand story doesn't change

Visual Consistency

- Colors match everywhere
- Typography is consistent
- Layouts share similar spacing
- Templates feel unified

Content Consistency

- Posts match our voice
- We educate regularly
- No random, off-brand content

Website Consistency

- Website matches our visual identity
- Messaging matches our social content
- Templates and layouts look aligned

Experience Consistency

- Customer communication follows standards
- Process is identical for all clients
- Our brand tone appears in emails and forms

SECTION 6 — USING YOUR AUDIT RESULTS

An audit is valuable only when paired with action.

Step 1: Identify your lowest-scoring areas

These are your high-priority weaknesses.

Examples:

- Website clarity
- Visual identity inconsistencies
- Weak testimonials
- Lack of content strategy
- Poor response times

Step 2: Separate Quick Wins from Major Projects

Quick Wins (Fix This Week)

- Update outdated info
- Fix broken links and images
- Add testimonials
- Align profile bios
- Compress images for speed
- Respond to old reviews
- Clean up navigation

Major Projects (Next 30–90 Days)

- Website redesign
- Brand refresh
- SEO overhaul
- Messaging framework update
- New photo or content strategy
- Automation setup

- System + process development

Step 3: Set Quarterly Improvement Goals

Example Quarterly Targets

Q1:
Improve Website Score from 22/40 to 30/40
– Fix speed
– Add CTAs
– Update copy

Q2:
Increase Trust Score from 10/40 to 22/40
– Collect 20+ new reviews
– Build case studies

Q3:
Boost Brand Consistency from 14/25 to 21/25
– Update all templates
– Align tone guidelines

Q4:
Strengthen Content Score
– Create consistent content pillars
– Post 3x per week

Step 4: Reaudit every 90 days

Each audit builds historical data showing:

- Growth
- Strengthened identity
- Improved clarity
- Elevated trust
- More aligned presence

Strong brands measure progress.
Weak brands assume it.

SECTION 7 — AUDIT ACTION PLAN TEMPLATE

(Keep this as your quarterly worksheet.)

Audit Date: _____

Scores:
50-Point Brand Audit: ___/50
Website Audit: ___/41
Digital Presence: ___/40 or ___/100
Brand Consistency: ___/25

Top 3 Weakest Areas:

1. _____
2. _____
3. _____

Immediate Actions (This Week):

☐ _____
☐ _____
☐ _____

Short-Term Fixes (This Month):

☐ _____
☐ _____
☐ _____

Long-Term Projects (Next 90 Days):

☐ _____
☐ _____
☐ _____

Next Audit Date: _____

SECTION 8 — WHEN TO HIRE HELP

Some issues are easy.
Some issues require professional support.

DIY-Friendly Fixes

- Updating website copy
- Responding to reviews
- Social posting
- Fixing broken links
- Updating images
- Basic SEO corrections
- Adding testimonials

Professional-Level Fixes

- Website redesign
- Complex SEO strategy
- Complete brand identity overhaul
- Photography and video production
- Automation setup
- Technical integrations
- Large-scale content strategy

If it is high-impact and outside your expertise, outsource it.

FINAL THOUGHT FOR THIS CHAPTER

Brands that audit themselves stay aligned, consistent, and credible.
They catch issues early, track performance, refine weak areas, and protect
their identity.

Brands that *don't* audit?

They drift.

Slowly. Quietly.
Until confusion replaces clarity, inconsistency replaces trust, and emotion
replaces strategy.

The Brand Audit Framework keeps your brand sharp, stable, and future-ready.
It ensures your identity grows with intention — not by accident.

Strong brands don't guess.
Strong brands measure.
Strong brands refine.
Strong brands stay aligned.

TEMPLATES & WORKSHEETS

Clarity is the foundation of every strong brand — and clarity begins with structure.

Every brand, at some point, reaches a moment where ideas start piling up. Messaging is floating in your head. Your purpose feels clear one day and unclear the next. Your audience shifts, your goals expand, and suddenly your brand feels bigger than what you can carry alone.

That's where templates and worksheets save you.

These tools pull your thoughts out of your mind and onto paper, turning scattered ideas into organized strategy. They help you articulate who you are, who you serve, how you communicate, and what you stand for. Without structure, branding becomes emotional. With structure, branding becomes intentional.

This chapter includes the **complete BrandNameSites Toolkit** — the same worksheets used internally during clarity sessions, brand discovery workshops, website planning meetings, and strategy intensives. These are practical, fill-in-the-blank templates designed to simplify your thinking and strengthen your brand.

You can use them as they are or customize them to your workflow. The format doesn't matter. The structure does.

A brand without structure drifts.
A brand with structure scales.

SECTION 1 — MISSION & VISION WORKSHEET

Your mission tells people what you do today.
Your vision tells them where you're going tomorrow.

Most small businesses confuse the two — or skip them entirely. But your mission and vision shape the long-term direction of your brand, your messaging, and your decisions.

Mission Statement Worksheet (Present Focus)

What do you do?

Who do you do it for?

What problem do you solve?

What makes your approach different?

What impact do you want to have right now?

Draft Your Mission Statement (1 sentence):

Vision Statement Worksheet (Future Focus)

Where is your brand going?

What future does your business create for your customers?

What impact will you make in 3–5 years?

What growth do you want to see?

Write Your Vision Statement (1–2 sentences):

SECTION 2 — AUDIENCE PERSONA WORKSHEET

You cannot speak clearly if you don't know who you're speaking to.

Personas help you understand exactly who your customer is, what they value, how they think, and what motivates their decisions.

Basic Profile

Persona Name (fictional):

Age Range:

Gender:

Location:

Occupation:

Income Level:

Education Level:

Psychographics (How they think and feel)

What do they value most?

_____

What frustrates them?

_____

What motivates them?

_____

What do they wish someone would explain simply?

_____

_____

Pain Points

- Pain Point 1:
  _____

- Pain Point 2:
  _____

- Pain Point 3:
  _____

_____

Goals

- Goal 1:
  _____

- Goal 2:
  _____

- Success Metrics: _____

_____

Behavior

Where do they spend their time online?

How do they research before buying?

What makes them trust a brand?

Who influences their decisions?

Persona Summary Sentence

(One line describing who they are)

SECTION 3 — MESSAGING FRAMEWORK

Your message must be recognizable, repeatable, and aligned.

This framework keeps your brand sounding like one unified voice — not fifty different versions of you.

Core Message

(The main idea you communicate everywhere)

Brand Promise

(What you guarantee your audience)

Value Pillars (Your 3–5 Main Points of Value)

1.
   o   Proof Point:

   _____

2.
   o   Proof Point:

   _____

3.
   o   Proof Point:

   _____

4.
   o   Proof Point:

   _____

Audience Benefit Statement

We help _____ achieve _____ so they can _____.

Signature Language

Phrases, tone, and language traits unique to your brand

Messaging Do & Don't List

DO say:

- _____
- _____

DON'T say:

- _____
- _____

SECTION 4 — BRAND IDENTITY WORKSHEET

Your brand identity isn't just visuals — it's personality, tone, and clarity.

Identity Basics

Purpose:

_____

Vision:

_____

Values (3–5):

1. _____
2. _____
3. _____
4. _____

_____

Brand Voice & Tone

Voice Description (3 words):

_____

Tone Style:
(Formal? Friendly? Motivational? Direct?)

_____
_____

Visual Identity

Primary Colors:

_____

Secondary Colors:

Typography:

- Headings: _____
- Body: _____

Imagery Style:

Spacing & Layout Guidelines:

Brand Personality (Choose 3–5)

☐ Confident
☐ Friendly
☐ Professional
☐ Educator
☐ Motivator
☐ Calm
☐ Direct
☐ Warm
☐ Creative
☐ Bold
☐ Minimalist
☐ Supportive
Other: _____

SECTION 5 — WEBSITE PLANNING FORM

A successful website is built on clarity — not creativity.

Use this form before designing or redesigning your website.

1. Website Goal

What is the #1 purpose of your website?

_____

_____

2. Homepage

Main Headline:

_____

Subheadline:

_____

Primary CTA:

_____

Three Key Highlights:

1. _____
2. _____
3. _____

_____

3. Services

List Your Services:

_____

Describe Each Service in One Sentence:

_____

_____

4. About Page

Short Introduction/Bio:

Why You Started This Business:

What Makes You Different:

5. Contact Page

Preferred Contact Method:

Expected Response Time:

Call-to-Action Statement:

6. Website Structure (Check All That Apply)

☐ Home
☐ About
☐ Services
☐ Portfolio
☐ Blog
☐ Contact
☐ Pricing
☐ FAQs
☐ Policies

SECTION 6 — CONTENT CALENDAR

Consistency is easier when you plan ahead.

Monthly Overview

Month: _____

Week-by-Week Planning

Week 1

Topic: _____
Platform(s): _____
Post Type: _____

Week 2

Topic: _____
Platform(s): _____
Post Type: _____

Week 3

Topic: _____
Platform(s): _____
Post Type: _____

Week 4

Topic: _____
Platform(s): _____
Post Type: _____

Content Notes

SECTION 7 — CONTENT CATEGORY WHEEL

This model helps you diversify content without losing consistency.

Draw a circle in the center labeled:
Your Core Brand Message

Around it, place 6–8 categories from the list below, or add your own.

Suggested Categories

- Education
- Authority / Expertise
- Behind the Scenes
- Storytelling
- Social Proof
- Offers & Services
- Personal Insight
- Industry Insight
- Community & Values

For each category, fill out:

Purpose of This Category:

Example Topics:

Preferred Formats (video, graphic, carousel, quote):

FINAL THOUGHT FOR THIS CHAPTER

Templates and worksheets are not busywork — they are the structural support beams of your brand. They transform the abstract into the actionable, the chaotic into the clear, and the overwhelming into the organized. They allow you to plan, refine, communicate, and scale without losing focus.

BUILT ON STANDARDS.

A brand without structure reacts.
A brand with structure leads.
And a brand that uses these worksheets becomes intentional, strategic, and unmistakably clear.

When you complete these templates, you don't just document your brand — you understand it.
You strengthen it.
You build it with purpose.

THE BRANDNAMESITES INDUSTRY STANDARDS

Standards don't exist to restrain you — they exist to protect you.

Most brands fail not because of lack of passion, creativity, or desire, but because they operate without rules. Each decision becomes emotional instead of strategic. Each new idea sends the brand in a different direction. Without structure, even a talented business becomes inconsistent. Without consistency, trust erodes.

BrandNameSites was built to solve exactly that problem — not by taking away creativity, but by giving it boundaries strong enough to support growth.

These industry standards define the **minimum level of professionalism** your brand must exhibit and the **maximum level of clarity** your audience deserves. They are simple enough for beginners to follow and deep enough for experts to respect. They serve as the guardrails for modern digital branding, ensuring your identity, visuals, messaging, and experience remain strong across every platform.

A brand with rules becomes trustworthy.
A brand with standards becomes unforgettable.

Below are the **official BrandNameSites Industry Standards** — the expectations, behaviors, and non-negotiables every brand must follow.

SECTION 1 — BASELINE RULES

These fundamental rules establish how every modern brand must operate. They are the foundation of the BrandNameSites philosophy and the principles that influence every design decision, every content choice, and every customer interaction.

Rule 1 — Clarity Before Creativity

A brand must be understood before it is admired.
If your customers don't understand what you do within seconds, no amount of creativity will save you. Cleverness is optional. Clarity is mandatory.

Rule 2 — One Message, Many Expressions

Your identity should be recognizable everywhere:
your website, your email signature, your social content, your captions, your ads.
The visuals can shift. The formats can vary. The tone can adapt.
But the **message** — the core of who you are — must remain the same.

Rule 3 — Everything Must Be Intentional

There is no room for "random."
No random colors.
No random captions.
No random posts.
Everything must serve a purpose connected to your brand strategy.

Rule 4 — Consistency Is Mandatory

People trust what they can predict.
When your brand tone, visuals, or behavior changes constantly, trust collapses.

Rule 5 — Simplicity Builds Strength

Your content, design, and user flow should be so simple that a visitor doesn't have to think twice.
Complexity confuses.
Simplicity converts.

Rule 6 — User Experience Comes First

If a design choice harms usability, it is not allowed — no matter how "cool" it looks.

Rule 7 — Your Website Is the Source of Truth

Your website is the home base.
Every message, offer, and identity element must align with the website.
Social media is rented space.
Your website is your property.

Rule 8 — Trends Cannot Lead the Brand

Trends fade. Brand equity lasts.
Your brand may participate in trends, but it must not be led by them.

Rule 9 — Consistency Over Perfection (Integrated from Version 2)

A consistent B+ brand beats an inconsistent A+ brand every time.
Your audience cares more about your reliability than your perfection.

Rule 10 — Data Over Intuition

Your instincts matter — but your data matters more.
Your analytics reveal the truth about what is working.

SECTION 2 — QUALITY EXPECTATIONS

BrandNameSites quality can be summarized simply:

If it does not build trust, it does not go live.

Quality is not just about looks — it's about clarity, accuracy, readability, and professionalism across every channel.

Below are the official expectations for modern branding and website work.

Quality Standard 1 — Clean, Intentional Layouts

- No clutter
- Strong visual hierarchy
- Spacing that breathes
- Logical flow from top to bottom
- Sections with clear purpose

A clean layout respects the user's time and attention.

Quality Standard 2 — Readable, Scannable Content

- Short sentences
- Predictable structure
- Clear headlines and subheadings
- Jargon-free language
- Skimmable paragraphs

Good branding guides the eye before it guides the mind.

Quality Standard 3 — Modern Visuals

- Consistent styling
- Clean color usage
- Modern typography
- Cohesive imagery
- Alignment with your brand personality

Modern does not mean trendy — it means **current, intentional, and timeless**.

Quality Standard 4 — Functional, Fast Experience

- Load times under 3 seconds
- Mobile-first design
- Clean navigation
- Functional buttons and forms
- No lag, no confusion

Slow equals unprofessional. Functionality is the backbone of credibility.

Quality Standard 5 — Professional Tone

Your brand should sound:

- Confident
- Clear
- Respectful
- Direct
- Authentic (not robotic, not overly casual)

Trust is built not just by what you say, but how you say it.

Quality Standard 6 — Trust Signals Are Required

You must include:

- Testimonials
- Reviews
- Case studies
- Credentials
- Client logos (if applicable)
- Clear processes
- Accessible contact options

Customers do not believe brands — they believe proof.

Quality Standard 7 — Authentic, Accurate Information (from Version 2)

Your content must be:

- Current
- Correct
- Transparent
- Honest

Outdated or vague information destroys trust faster than anything else.

SECTION 3 — VISUAL STANDARDS

Visual consistency separates professional brands from amateur ones. These standards ensure that what you show the world is unmistakably *you* — everywhere.

Color Standards

- Use primary colors intentionally
- Use secondary colors sparingly
- Maintain consistency across platforms
- Avoid neon or distracting tones unless part of your brand
- Maintain required contrast for accessibility
- Document hex codes, RGB, and CMYK

Color is not decoration — it is identity.

Typography Standards

- One heading font
- One body font
- Clear hierarchy (H1 → H2 → H3 → body)
- No decorative fonts for body text
- Minimum 16px body size (accessibility requirement)
- Clear documentation of font usage and weights

Typography is the voice of your visuals.

Spacing Standards

- Generous padding
- Balanced margins
- Consistent spacing between elements
- 4px or 8px base spacing system
- No cramped layouts
- No forced-alignment issues

White space is a design element, not empty space.

Imagery Standards

- Use cohesive tones and styles
- High-resolution images only
- Avoid corporate, generic stock photos
- Consistent photo treatment/color grading
- Represent your brand personality visually

Images should feel like part of one world — your world.

Template Standards

- Use approved templates for social, web, and email
- Maintain the hierarchy (title → subtitle → body → CTA)
- Never break templates without strategic reason
- Use consistent layout structures

Templates create efficiency and recognizable patterns.

SECTION 4 — DIGITAL BEHAVIOR STANDARDS

How your brand **acts online** is just as important as how it **looks**. These standards guide your digital behavior across websites, social media, email, advertising, and customer interactions.

Standard 1 — Fast Response Times

Respond to inquiries within **24–48 hours**.
Slow response signals disorganization and damages credibility.

Standard 2 — Professional Interactions

All communication should be:

- Clear
- Respectful
- Consistent
- On-brand

Customers should feel guided, not confused.

Standard 3 — Consistent Posting Rhythm

Consistency beats frequency.
Not daily.
Not random.
Just predictable.

Standard 4 — Purpose-Driven Content

Every piece of content must serve one of these functions:

- Educate
- Inform
- Connect
- Convert
- Build trust

Anything outside these purposes does not belong on your platform.

Standard 5 — No Off-Brand Behavior

If it contradicts your values, tone, or identity, it is not allowed — anywhere.

Standard 6 — Protect the Customer Experience

Avoid:

- Sudden changes
- Confusing offers
- Unclear pricing
- Random shifts in messaging

A predictable journey builds long-term loyalty.

Standard 7 — Show Up the Same Everywhere

Your brand must feel unified across:

- Website
- Social media
- Email
- Ads
- Reviews
- Messaging

Multi-platform consistency signals maturity.

Standard 8 — Maintain a Clean Digital Footprint

- Remove outdated posts
- Update old information
- Delete abandoned profiles
- Fix inconsistent messaging

Your digital footprint tells customers who you are — clean it regularly.

Standard 9 — User-Centric Thinking (Integrated from Version 2)

Everything you create should consider how real users experience it — not how *you* think it should work.

SECTION 5 — NON-NEGOTIABLES

These rules are absolute. They are not optional, not flexible, and not debatable. They are the BrandNameSites non-negotiables required to build a credible, modern brand.

Non-Negotiable 1 — Mobile-First Websites

More than 60% of users browse on mobile.
If your mobile layout is weak, your brand is weak.
Everything must work flawlessly on smartphones.

Non-Negotiable 2 — Clarity on Every Page

Every page must answer:

- What is this?
- Why does it matter?
- What's the next step?

Confusion kills conversions.

Non-Negotiable 3 — Consistent Branding

No inconsistent fonts, colors, tones, or visuals — ever.

Non-Negotiable 4 — Professional Copywriting

Your words must be structured, purposeful, and clear.
No filler.
No fluff.
No confusion.

Non-Negotiable 5 — Fast Load Times

Slow equals unprofessional.
Every second counts.

Non-Negotiable 6 — Trust Signals Must Be Visible

A brand without social proof looks untested and untrustworthy.

Non-Negotiable 7 — Updated Information Only

Outdated information instantly damages credibility.

Non-Negotiable 8 — Predictable User Experience

Users must always know where they are and what to do next.

Non-Negotiable 9 — Privacy and Security

Secure forms, SSL certificates, proper policies — no exceptions.

Non-Negotiable 10 — Standards Before Creativity

Standards are the foundation.
Creativity is the expression.

SECTION 6 — FUTURE-PROOFING STANDARDS

Technology changes. Trends evolve. Platforms rise and fall.
But strong brands stay relevant because they prepare for the future.

These standards help you build a brand that survives the next decade — not just the next trend.

Future-Proofing Standard 1 — Build for Longevity, Not Trends

Trends are temporary.
Standards endure.

Future-Proofing Standard 2 — Update Quarterly

Quarterly audits prevent outdated information, outdated designs, and outdated experiences.

Future-Proofing Standard 3 — Optimize for AI & Search

Structure your content so it is:

- Easy to index
- Easy to understand
- Easy for AI tools to reference
- Answer-based and clear

Clarity fuels both human and machine comprehension.

Future-Proofing Standard 4 — Own Your Digital Home

Own your:

- Hosting
- Domain
- Website
- Content

Your digital home must always be under your control.

Future-Proofing Standard 5 — Create Systems That Scale

- Templates
- Workflows
- Automations
- Standardized communication

Systems create freedom.
Systems create consistency.
Systems create scale.

Future-Proofing Standard 6 — Teach Before You Sell

Education builds trust.
Trust builds loyalty.
Loyalty builds longevity.

Future-Proofing Standard 7 — Build a Recognizable Identity

Recognition outlasts algorithms.

Future-Proofing Standard 8 — Remain Customer-Centered

Platforms will change.
Algorithms will change.
Technology will change.
Human needs will not.
Serve the human, not the trend.

FINAL THOUGHT FOR THIS CHAPTER

Industry standards are not creative restrictions — they are brand insurance. They protect your integrity, your clarity, your professionalism, and the customer experience you've worked hard to build.

When you follow these standards:

- You don't chase trends — you outlive them.
- You don't blend in — you stand apart.
- You don't confuse people — you guide them.
- You don't rebuild from scratch — you evolve with intention.

This is what makes the BrandNameSites system different.
It is not about building a brand.
It is about building a **standard** —
a standard strong enough to shape your business, your presence, and your future.

CLOSING REFLECTIONS & THE BRANDNAMESITES PHILOSOPHY

Branding is not a moment.
It is not a trend.
It is not a logo, a color palette, or a clever phrase.

Branding is discipline — a living system shaped by clarity, consistency, and structure. If this book has shown you anything, it is that branding is not built in a day. It is built in the daily decisions, the small refinements, the commitment to standards, and the steady choice to show up with intention.

Throughout every chapter, every framework, every worksheet, and every standard, one message has remained constant:

A strong brand is built on standards.

Not assumptions.
Not guesswork.
Not scattered effort.

Standards.

The BrandNameSites philosophy was created because too many entrepreneurs feel lost in the maze of modern branding. They feel overwhelmed by design trends, confused by conflicting advice, pressured to be perfect, and unsure what truly matters.

This philosophy clears the fog.
It brings structure to the chaos.
It gives you rules that free you, not restrict you.

Below are the core principles that define the BrandNameSites way — principles that will guide you long after you close this book.

1. Clarity Is the Foundation

Clarity is not optional.
Clarity is oxygen.

If people do not understand you quickly, they cannot trust you. And if they cannot trust you, they will not buy from you — no matter how talented you are or how beautiful your visuals may be.

Clarity touches every part of your brand:

- your message
- your website
- your visuals
- your content
- your emails
- your processes
- your customer experience

Clarity is not a paragraph you write once.
Clarity is something you protect every day.

2. Consistency Builds Trust

Brands decay in inconsistency.
They collapse when the tone changes every month.
They lose credibility when the visuals shift constantly.
They confuse their audience when the message is unstable.

Consistency is how trust is built — slowly, predictably, intentionally.

Consistency is:

- visual
- verbal
- digital
- behavioral
- experiential

When you show up the same way everywhere, people feel safe choosing you. And in the digital world, trust is currency.

A consistent brand becomes recognizable.
A recognizable brand becomes chosen.

3. Structure Creates Strength

Many people misunderstand structure. They think it limits creativity. But structure is actually what gives creativity freedom — because it removes chaos.

A brand without structure eventually collapses under its own weight.
A brand built on systems becomes durable, scalable, and stable.

Structure gives you:

- organization
- predictability
- workflow
- clarity
- scalability
- ease

The systems in this book — worksheets, frameworks, audits, templates, scorecards, and standards — are the backbone of long-term brand strength.

Structure does not restrict you.
Structure empowers you.

4. Your Website Is Your Center

In a world of disappearing platforms, shifting algorithms, and unpredictable social networks, your website remains the one place that is truly yours.

It is:

- your headquarters
- your home base
- your digital storefront
- your brand's proof of seriousness
- your most important asset

Every chapter in this book returns to the same truth:

All roads lead back to your website.

When your website is strong, your brand becomes strong.
When your website is weak, your brand feels shaky everywhere — even on social media.

Your website is not a trend.
It is your foundation.

5. Branding Is Discipline

Most people treat branding like a project.
It is not.

Branding is a discipline — a daily practice of alignment and intention.

Discipline means:

- staying consistent even when it's easier not to
- refining regularly
- keeping your website updated
- maintaining your content rhythm
- protecting your message
- following your standards
- showing up with professionalism

The brands that lose momentum are not the ones who lack talent.
They are the ones who lose discipline.

The brands that win are the ones who maintain it.

6. Simplicity Wins

Simplicity is power. It cuts through noise, overload, and distraction.

Simple does not mean basic.
Simple means strong, intentional, and clear.

Simple brands communicate better.
Simple brands convert better.
Simple brands are easier to remember.

Simplicity must show up everywhere:

- simple content
- simple calls-to-action
- simple layouts
- simple navigation
- simple messaging
- simple design decisions

The world is already crowded.
Your brand should rise above the chaos — not add to it.

FINAL REFLECTION

This chapter closes your learning.
But your work begins now.

Everything in this book means nothing without application.
Every framework, every standard, every worksheet becomes powerful only
when you use it.

Branding is not something you launch.
Branding is something you live.

You now have:

- a philosophy
- a system
- a standard
- a structure
- a roadmap
- a method
- a discipline

The rest depends on your consistency.

When you apply the principles you've learned — not just once, but repeatedly — your brand will not only grow…

it will lead.

CONCLUSION

You've come to the end of this book, but you are standing at the beginning of a new level of clarity, confidence, and direction. You now have the structure most businesses never receive — a complete, modern framework to build, maintain, and scale a brand in today's digital world.

This is not a goodbye.
This is a recommitment to discipline.

Recommit to Brand Consistency

Your brand is only as strong as your commitment to keep it aligned.

Recommit to:

- showing up clearly
- maintaining your visuals
- protecting your message
- updating your website
- posting with intention
- honoring your standards
- following your systems
- choosing clarity over complexity

Consistency is not perfection.
Consistency is aligned behavior over time.

When you are consistent, people learn to trust you.
When people trust you, they choose you.

Encourage Application

You do not need to fix everything at once.
Start with your biggest gap:

- Is it your website?
- Your content?
- Your voice?
- Your visuals?
- Your process?
- Your user journey?
- Your digital footprint?
- Your trust signals?

Pick one area.
Strengthen it.
Measure it.
Then move to the next.

Use the worksheets.
Follow the frameworks.
Return to the audits.
Repeat the standards.

Application builds results.
Discipline keeps them.

Final Words on Digital Discipline

This book was not written to impress you.
It was written to equip you.

Digital branding is not chaotic when you understand the rules.
It is not overwhelming when you have structure.
It is not confusing when you follow standards.

Digital discipline means:

- protecting clarity
- maintaining quality
- honoring systems
- refining consistently
- staying aligned
- staying intentional
- staying focused

In a world full of noise, digital discipline is your advantage.
It is what separates brands that fade from brands that last.

You now have everything you need to build a brand that stands firm —
a brand people trust, remember, and choose.

The work continues beyond this page.
And now, you have the standards to guide you.

Build with clarity.
Grow with consistency.
Lead with intention.
And let your brand speak with strength — every day.

BRANDNAMESITES SYSTEM SUPPORT

This section exists to support everything you've learned in this book. It is the companion section that reinforces your branding discipline with definitions, tools, worksheets, platforms, and recommended systems.

This section turns theory into action.

It is designed for real-world execution — the same tools used by BrandNameSites internally and the same structure we use to guide clients through clarity, consistency, and long-term brand discipline.

GLOSSARY — KEY TERMS IN MODERN BRANDING

Aesthetic
The overall "look and feel" of your brand visuals — mood, tone, style, color, layout.

Audit
A structured, systematic review of your brand, website, or digital presence to measure alignment and performance.

Authority
Your perceived expertise based on value-driven content, clarity, consistency, and trust signals.

Brand Identity
Your complete system of visuals, voice, values, personality, and expression.

Brand Positioning
The unique space you occupy in the market — and how customers perceive your value.

Brand Standards
The non-negotiable rules that protect consistency across platforms.

Call-to-Action (CTA)
A specific instruction that tells the user what to do next.

Case Study
A proof document showing a client's problem, your process, and the results delivered.

Clarity
The ability for someone to understand your brand instantly. The foundation of every chapter in this book.

CMS
Content Management System — the platform where your website pages live and are edited.

Content Identity
How your brand sounds through content — tone, message, consistency.

Content Strategy
Your structured plan for creating content that educates, positions, and supports your brand.

Conversion
A completed action (purchase, booking, download, inquiry).

Core Web Vitals
Google's official metrics for evaluating website performance and user experience.

Digital Footprint
Every online trace of your brand — your website, social, reviews, listings, content, and SEO presence.

Digital Presence
The complete picture of what the world sees about your brand online.

Funnel
A guided path that moves users from awareness → interest → action.

Hub & Spoke Model
BrandNameSites' system where your website is the hub, and all other marketing platforms are spokes.

Messaging Framework
Your structured system for voice, tone, language, value pillars, and positioning.

Persona
A fictional representation of your ideal customer.

SEO (Search Engine Optimization)
Improving website and content visibility in search engines.

Social Proof
Evidence that real people trust and value your brand.

User Journey
The path customers take from discovering you → understanding you → choosing you.

UX (User Experience)
How users feel navigating your website or digital environment.

Visual Identity
Your brand's colors, fonts, imagery, spacing, and design system.

TOOLS & RESOURCES — THE BRANDNAMESITES TOOLKIT

Below is the curated list of tools referenced throughout the book — aligned with the BrandNameSites philosophy of clarity, consistency, and structured execution.

Branding Tools

- **Canva Pro** — Templates, brand kits, layouts
- **Figma** — Professional UI/UX and design systems
- **Coolors / Adobe Color** — Color exploration
- **Google Fonts** — Free, professional typography
- **Frontify** — Brand guideline hosting

Website Tools

- **Webflow** — Modern, responsive, clean
- **WordPress + Elementor** — Flexible and widely supported
- **Vercel** — High-performance hosting
- **Supabase** — Backend + database
- **Shopify** — E-commerce systems
- **Google Analytics** — Traffic and behavior
- **Ahrefs / SEMRush** — SEO

Content & Workflow Tools

- **Notion** — Content planning
- **Airtable** — Content and asset organization
- **Trello / Asana** — Workflow tracking
- **Meta Business Suite** — IG/FB scheduling
- **Descript** — Video/audio editing
- **CapCut** — Reels and short-form content

Brand Maintenance Tools

- **Google Business Profile**
- **Checkbot** — Browser-based audit
- **Pingdom / GTMetrix** — Site speed scoring
- **Hotjar** — Heatmaps + user behavior
- **Google Search Console** — Indexing + search health

RECOMMENDED TECH STACK — THE BRANDNAMESITES SYSTEM

This tech stack aligns directly with the methods, frameworks, and standards taught across the book.

1. Website Tech Stack

- **Webflow** (primary)
- **WordPress + Elementor** (secondary option)
- **Vercel** (hosting for custom builds)
- **Supabase** (database & backend)
- **Cloudflare** (security + caching)

2. Branding & Design Stack

- Canva Pro
- Figma
- Adobe Express
- Unsplash / Pexels (photos)

3. Content Creation Stack

- CapCut
- Descript
- Notion
- Meta Business Suite
- ChatGPT

4. Business & Communication Stack

- Google Workspace
- Zoom / Google Meet
- Stripe / PayPal
- Calendly
- HubSpot

5. Monitoring & Maintenance Stack

- GTMetrix
- Checkbot
- Hotjar
- Google Search Console

This stack supports the full BrandNameSites system — from clarity → structure → scaling.

BOOK INDEX

(Generated after your final layout is exported.)

Suggested index terms include:

Once the manuscript is final, export to Word and use Word's indexing tool to create cross-referenced entries.

ATTRIBUTION OF EXTERNAL SOURCES

This book is fully original, but references common tools and platforms used widely across the digital branding industry:

- Webflow
- WordPress
- Google Analytics
- Google Business Profile
- Coolors
- Adobe Color
- Canva
- Figma
- Supabase
- Shopify

No copyrighted material is reproduced.
All references are descriptive, not quoted.

If future editions include visuals or tutorials, platform-specific attribution may be required.

BONUS DOWNLOADS — OFFICIAL BRANDNAMESITES RESOURCES

These downloads expand the value of the book and help readers apply the BrandNameSites standards immediately.

Included PDF Downloads

- Brand Identity Worksheet
- Website Planning Form
- Messaging Framework
- Audience Persona Worksheet
- Monthly + Weekly Content Calendar
- Content Category Wheel
- Quarterly Brand Audit Checklist
- 50-Point Brand Audit

Templates

- Homepage Layout Template
- Services Page Structure
- About Page Guide
- Contact Page Conversion Template
- Brand Standards Snapshot
- Hub & Spoke Traffic Map

Tools

- Brand Maintenance Planner
- Industry Standards Quick Guide
- Funnel Flowcharts (Starter → Advanced)

Optional Premium Add-Ons

- Fillable PDF versions
- Notion templates
- Webflow starter project
- Canva brand kit templates
- AI content prompt library
- Automated website audit sheet

These elevate the book into a full execution system.

FINAL THOUGHT FOR THE BACK MATTER

This book does not end with ideas — it ends with the tools required to turn ideas into execution.

Your advantage is clarity.
Your strength is structure.
Your power is consistency.
Your growth will come from discipline.

Whenever your brand feels unclear, unfocused, or misaligned — return to the standards.

BrandNameSites has given you the system.
Now, you build the standard others will follow.

ABOUT THE AUTHOR

Collectively as a team, we set our minds on end goal results for people that don't have the time to research and the knowledge to apply to mutually meet us at the middle of the road. We utilized our experience from the lack of knowledge in empathizing with others who may fall short of their goals, or stumble to prevent a fall.

NOTES

BUILT ON STANDARDS.

BUILT ON STANDARDS.

www.ingramcontent.com/pod-product-compliance
Lightning Source LLC
Chambersburg PA
CBHW061242220326
41599CB00028B/5513